THE TRANSFORMATIONAL PATH

HOW HEALING, UNLEARNING, AND TUNING INTO SOURCE HELPED ME MANIFEST MY MOST ABUNDANT LIFE

CLAUDIA AMENDOLA ALZRAA

The Transformational Path.

Copyright © Claudia Amendola Alzraa, 2023

First Edition

ISBN (paperback) 978-1-914447-78-5

ISBN (ebook) 978-1-914447-79-2

All rights reserved. No part of this book may be reproduced in any form, including photocopying and recording, without permission in writing from the publisher, except for brief quotes in review or reference.

This book contains information for entertainment purposes only and should not be used as a substitute for professional medical advice. It is always advisable to consult a medical professional.

Although every effort has been made to ensure the accuracy of the information in this book, no responsibility is assumed for any loss, damage, or disruption caused by errors or omissions, and no liability is assumed for any damages caused by its use.

The views expressed in this book are those of the author alone and do not reflect those of TGH International Ltd.

This book is a work of creative nonfiction, however, certain elements may have been fictionalized in varying degrees, for various purposes to suit the narrative.

Prepared by TGH International Ltd.

www.TGHBooks.com

This book is for my son, Raphaël. I am endlessly grateful that all my decisions along my journey lead me to your wonderful father and brought you into my life. Thank you for all the lessons and karmic healing. Thank you for choosing me and making me a Mom. I cannot wait to see what stories you write for yourself as you grow.
I love you with all of my being.

ACKNOWLEDGMENTS

Thank you to my husband, Jordan, for calling me a "writer" from the first day we met, and continuously supporting this dream of mine. You were my number one supporter throughout my authorship journey, and I am your number one supporter throughout all of life.

Thank you to my parents, Marisa and Ugo, who raised a reader and a passionate writer. Thank you for always telling me that I had, "a way with words" and for giving me wings to fly and follow my dreams.

Thank you to my brother, Anthony, for being the best cheerleader and my best friend. Thank you to my sister-in-law, Andrea, for being right there alongside him, joining in the cheering.

Thank you to my soul sister, Nataskia, for being the first person to ever read this book. I am endlessly grateful that spending time in Paris also led me to you.

Thank you to my spiritual advisor, Carol Righton, and to all my soul family at Akasha's Den in Oakville; I can still remember the first time I walked through your doors during Midnight Madness, and my spirit was forever shaken.

Thank you to my son, Raphaël, for changing my life, and for Awakening the creative energy in me that helped birth this book.

Thank you to Karen and Sean at The Good House for believing in me and my story.

Thank you to all who have made a ripple in my life in some way.

Thank you to you, reader, for helping this dream come true.

"For a true writer, each book should be a new beginning where he tries again for something that is beyond attainment. He should always try for something that has never been done or that others have tried and failed. Then sometimes, with great luck, he will succeed."

- *Ernest Hemingway*

CONTENTS

Introduction	xi
1. Comfortable is Not a Synonym for Abundant	1
2. What Acceptance Looks Like	39
3. What Risk Looks Like	63
4. Fairy Tales Are Real	87
5. Don't Stop Believing	125
6. Spiritual Lessons and Channeled Downloads	157
7. Life, Now - My Thoughts on Motherhood	213
Our Stories Never Truly End	233
About the Author	237

INTRODUCTION

As a young child, my parents always used to say to me, "You can have everything you want in life - so long as you truly believe in it and work hard for it."

Most people never hear the end of that sentence which triggers a complete misunderstanding of the power of manifesting, right from childhood.

We are usually told (and sold by spiritual gurus) that, "If you believe in something hard enough, it will come true."

We head forward into life wishing, hoping, praying, and dreaming that what we want will fall into our laps. We don't work for it, we expect it, and we scorn the Universe when it doesn't happen for us. However, with all life - and all manifesting - the second half of my

INTRODUCTION

parents' advice is the most important... *You need to work hard for what you want.*

Working hard looks different all the time, depending on what it is you are working towards. Yet, I can tell you without an ounce of hesitation, that everything I've wanted in life, I ended up getting. With work. And a lot of work, at that.

I am a psychic medium with clairvoyant and clairaudient gifts but, aside from all that, I have the amazing ability to truly *pull* all that my life needs towards me. Do you notice how I said *need* and not *want*, this time around?

That's another issue that complicates the process of manifesting - not being able to define what you need separate from what you think the world wants of you. This creates a soul distortion that will have you wondering why you got what you hoped for, but will still have you continuing to search for more.

None of this process is easy. In fact, it's often paired with a scoop of suffering and a dash of struggle, but it's worth it in the end because the joy that pairs with successful manifestation is immeasurable.

My spiritual companions often refer to me as a *Super Manifestor*. They say I'm the one "living the dream." That's what successful manifesting is: being able to turn those dreams into your reality and daily life.

Those who are closest to me find that I seem to

INTRODUCTION

naturally draw in the good jujus in their life when they're around me. They call me a lucky rabbit's foot. It's merely because they are learning my manifestation behaviours through my character and demeanor. As such, they begin to emulate it themselves, and see the results of *proper manifestation*. Proper manifestation is the ability to identify what changes in your life are needed to bring you the most joy, and the act of actually working towards implementing those changes into your reality.

I believe that absolutely everyone has the ability to become infinitely happy and manifest the truly wonderful life they envision for themselves. I also believe that everyone deserves the kind of abundance that fulfills all aspects of a person's life; I am referring to emotional abundance, mental abundance, physical abundance, financial abundance and, most importantly, spiritual abundance.

However, before that happens, there are many aspects to manifesting that need to be unlearned, many mindsets that need to be shifted, so much healing that needs to happen and many definitions of abundance that need to be redefined. This is the reason I wrote this book.

I hope that my experiences, my lessons, my downfalls, and my growth will be the inspiration for others to also grab hold of their life and turn it into a fairy tale. I want people to learn, through my magnetism, how to also become Super Manifestors, and to manifest

INTRODUCTION

the life they deserve: the life that the Universe truly wants them to live.

And the key to all this is to transform your life, to heal yourself completely, and to step into action and grab the life you want by the horns.

A FEW NOTES ABOUT THE CONTENT IN THIS BOOK

First and foremost, I am a spiritual being and not a religious one. I learn from and value many religions, but my practice is suited to the relationship I have formed with what is greater than me. All my spiritual practice is Light and Love energy centered.

That being said, I am not a, "Just think positive thoughts," practitioner. I merely seek to work with energies that vibrate higher than I do. My life goal is to rise and I cannot do that if I'm working with dark, earth-bound, or ego-driven energies; I don't commune with ghosts, I don't do spellwork and I don't ask for the help of deities that hurt or curse others. I work with angels, archangels, Ascended Masters, and God.

You may find that I use the words God, Source, or Universe within this book. I use them interchangeably and I want you to mentally adjust what you read to suit your comfort level, as well. When I say God, Source, or Universe, I am referring to the overarching energy of

INTRODUCTION

Love that brings order to the chaos. I am referring to that Zen state. I am referring to the Enlightenment that the Buddhists speak of. I am referring to Christ Consciousness. I am referring to YWHA - the name the Jewish people gave to their Lord. I am referring to the Divine Source of All. I am referring to *something* that vibrates higher than everything else.

This is the energy we should all strive to align with in order to find that abundance we deserve. Aligning to that energy means that everything we are are doing and saying comes from a place of Love. We are living *Love* and performing all actions selflessly and with the betterment of the planet in mind.

The energy of Love is within all of us and flows through all of us. It is what the Christians refer to as, "Being made in the image of God."

You cannot escape it; you are One with it.

I'm here to help you uncap this well because it springs eternal in everyone, and it is evidence of how powerful, important, and transcendent you truly are.

Secondly, you may see me refer to my guides or angels and archangels in this text. As I said, I only converse with and work with Beings of Light - those which vibrate on the energy of Love as well. Working with Higher Beings is not necessary to successfully manifesting the life you deserve.

You should use my experiences and advice as you see

INTRODUCTION

fit, and mold what I say and suggest to suit your spiritual comfort level. Work with who you are comfortable with, but know that they are available to you if you need them.

My only advice is to keep it Light(-centered)! Keeping it with the angels, archangels, Ascended Masters, and saints is where you want to be. Anything else will only provide you short-term joy and long-term ego issues. You want to get to that high-rising spot (you deserve it!), so seek out a bond with Beings already at that energetic level. The easiest way to ensure you're communing with "the right dudes" is to monitor how your ego reacts to this connection; if you feel all wise and powerful, it's time to re-evaluate your team.

Finally, nothing within my spiritual practice (or in this book) has a "set it and forget it" approach. If you're not ready to put in the work, if you're not prepared to heal, if you're not willing to unlearn, if you're not going to make the tough decisions and take the risks, this book isn't for you.

The path to abundance, the journey to joy, is not an easy one... Sometimes it really sucks! Yet, as with all ebbs and flows in life, it ends up being *so* worth it.

Remember, I am by no means an authority figure on how the Universe wants or expects things. I am a messenger. And, like with all messengers, feel free to approach my words with discernment. Choose what resonates best with you and leave what doesn't. A

INTRODUCTION

message is not wrong just because it doesn't *all* jive with you. Truth can be hidden in the strangest places, after all.

I ask that you be honest with yourself. If something really triggers you, or rubs you up the wrong way, more often than not there is a mirror being held up to you and some healing that needs to happen. In my youth, I often found that the comments and ideas that made me the angriest were the ones I was not ready to hear - but certainly needed to.

Are you ready to change your life?

Abundance is your birthright, so let's walk the path of transformation, together.

"Never confuse movement with action."

- Ernest Hemingway

CHAPTER ONE
COMFORTABLE IS NOT A SYNONYM FOR ABUNDANT

Ever since I was a small child growing up in Canada, I have always felt pretty lucky. I was always aware of my connection to something greater than myself. I used this awareness to write, wish, hope, and pray to God for things I needed. Rather, I asked for what kids think they need, which is mostly learned from their parents (or sugar and toy related, let's be real).

Now, when you're a kid, working hard for what you want means being a good little girl. So, I would put my desires into the Universe, focus hard on my school work, get the good grades, be polite to my brother, and things seemed to fall into place. I felt the rewards of working hard. I always seemed to get *what I was told that I needed* by my parents and by authority figures, such as teachers.

That was the beginning of the "manifestation mix-up," as I like to call it - I learned what I needed from others. I defined what would make me happy along the lines of what others thought happiness and satisfaction were. As I grew up, this meant that I felt that the life I needed to work hard towards followed the traditional standard that was aspired for me: a university degree, a relationship, a steady and respectable job, a house, and a car. Because, of course, the key to happiness follows this neat and organized path, *right?*

Wrong.

Now, I'll be honest with you, I got it all. I got everything I thought I wanted because I was taught I needed it. I had it drop into my lap with just a little bit of work on my part, or sometimes with the help from my parents; none of that "hard work" my mom and dad talked about when I was growing up. All these milestones took minimal effort, seemingly manifesting on their own after a few discussions with my parents about my (their) plans for my future and the next steps needed by me.

I got the brand new car as I headed into high school graduation. I graduated on the Honor Roll despite skipping 90 percent of my university classes, because I was using those missed classes to be far ahead of classmates on my essay writing. I was the first to apply to employment searches and I got a steady job in teaching before the majority of my colleagues from university. I was able to buy myself a house the moment that permanent contract appeared in my lap (and before the market exploded) - something that was continuously pushed as a definition of success in Ontario, Canada. What's more, I was in a pretty serious relationship with someone I had known for many years prior; familiarity means less risk after all.

I believe the ease at which all this seemed to come to me was deliberate as one of my toughest lessons from the Universe. You may roll your eyes while reading that and call me out, saying, "Claudia, people who have it harder learn far more than you who had everything drop into her lap!"

But I disagree... at least for me.

It's true; when you are uncomfortable with your life and are unhappy with the circumstances, there is a great drive to change it. In most situations, you will fight tooth and nail to transform this, which develops strength and resilience. I don't believe those were the characteristics I needed in the moments of my life previously mentioned.

As an individual who believes in past lives (I'll talk more about this later), I do feel as though the start of this reincarnation was not meant to be a struggle. That would come later on.

I feel that, at that stage in my life, I was meant to navigate what I was manifesting for myself and what I was manifesting because it was expected of me by others.

I believe I was meant to look at the lot I was handed in life and carefully assess whether I was defining it according to what I thought I wanted or what I really needed. I also believe this is something I was unable to do in past lives, and I continuously returned to the soul realm having not learned the lesson of "live for yourself and your joy and the rest of life will fall into place."

When you are comfortable and everything seems to be going swimmingly, when you aren't struggling day-to-day, when your life seems to unfold exactly how everyone else told you it should, why fight it, *right?*

Who wants to leave comfortable?

I imagine it to be much like the snug and safe womb of a mother. As a baby do you really want to leave that space and start your life screaming in the harsh realities of the real world? Probably not!

You've got someone nourishing you, you're warm, you're protected, and you don't need to make any harsh decisions because life is carefully laid out for you by someone else. Comfortable bliss!

To leave that sheltered space means you have to:

- Start all over again and rebuild the foundation of your life
- Lose a lot, in order to gain potentially nothing
- Give up everything you have established as your own, including what others saw as your successes
- Work harder, when you were getting nice and comfortable in the security of this routine
- Disappoint everyone else in the process of making this change

I was making steady money. I was living a life with very few struggles, financially. I was burying all my mental illnesses under the mask of what a successful life is supposed to look like. I reached the milestones I was told growing up, that I needed to hit before thirty. And I wasn't alone, which added another layer of protection to my infinite pile of facades.

I thought I had manifested everything I could need with just a little bit of intention and a side of light work. It was easier than my parents had told me it would be! Except I was completely and utterly unhappy. Despite building this picture-perfect standard of the life that people longed for me, I was empty and unsatisfied. Something was wrong... This wasn't *it*.

LIFE IS NOT A CHECKLIST

I viewed the entirety of my life as a checklist and, unfortunately, viewed all people as either a hindrance to completing that next checklist item or as a tool that could get me there. Quite honestly, I didn't really value anyone unless they served a purpose in hitting these "milestones."

When you view life as an endless race made up of a compilation of checkpoints, the present becomes of very little importance. When you hit a checkpoint, immediately, your mind is on the next flag that needs to be captured. You are never living in the moment and never truly taking time to appreciate each success that you have reached.

When a person is living in a milestone race, especially one that is set by external sources, they are truly never happy. Take it from me, there was no moment of gratitude or appreciation, and no pat on the back to myself when I was accomplishing these things in my life. Instead, my mind immediately fixated on, "What's next?"

If you are living with a *"what's next?"* approach to life, you will never be satisfied. You devalue what success truly is and you are not taking a moment to thank God for what has just transpired in your life. If you aren't living a life of gratitude, eventually the joy stops, and eventually the blessings become blocked. It's a fact of the spiritual life.

This checklist outlook actually hinders manifesting in the long run. You are telling the Universe that you haven't established clarity on what it is you need to feel happy in your life, because you are seemingly always wanting more. I missed so many small joys and mini successes along my path because I was so focused on "the big things". I was never really, truly happy because I always thought there was another goal I needed to accomplish before I could be happy.

Unfortunately, in our social media driven world, only "the big things" seem to matter to everyone else, and so we place a greater worth on those milestones and become more obsessed with completing that checklist. This all comes back to the concept of allowing our joy to be defined by external sources, rather than what we spiritually need to thrive.

And, of course, that race never actually ends. There is no finish line to cross when you are living in this state of mind. You are just endlessly running and, eventually, all people burn out.

I was burnt out.

FINANCIAL DISSATISFACTION IN A SAFE SPACE

I had what others would define as a great, secure job. I had an impressive salary that allowed me to pay bills without any issues. I was also already paying into one of the best retirement pension plans in Canada, and I had money to spare. Most people would look at a teacher's salary in Ontario and say that it's impressive.

In spite of that, I was completely dissatisfied, financially.

The primary cause of this dissatisfaction was because I associated success with monetary wealth, and so I was continuously fearful of losing it. I watched the numbers in my bank account like a hawk watches its prey. I had panic attacks when I needed to pull from savings. When I was spending on things that "other people wouldn't see," such as home repairs and car related issues, I would get anxious about the loss of this money. I feared losing money and monitored the prices on menus and the cost of vacations with obsessive behaviour.

And yet, at the same time, I was overspending on stupid stuff to fill the void. I was squandering my money in places that really didn't matter because I thought:

- It's a small purchase and won't impact my overall wealth

- It will make me happy in the moment
- It will take up space in the emptiness of my spirit
- People see "things" and that is associated with having money to spare

I managed to acquire a collection of the most random junk that was just taking up shelf space, collecting dust, and making a mess of my house. I didn't reflect on these little things I was buying because I felt in control when it was small and manageable. The temporary joy it gave me, until I went on to buy another little thing, was what I needed to quench my thirst for happiness. It was like drinking drops of water in a desert storm.

The other issue which influenced my dissatisfaction was that I never really established a clear definition of what "wealth" was supposed to look like. Instead, I correlated it to the milestones I was hitting. That correlation meant that, like my small successes, I was not celebrating my small financial joys. I was not taking time to thank the Universe for my monetary blessings, such as the ability to pay my bills or being able to buy a coffee in the morning. Instead, I was wasting it on stupid junk and hoarding it in all other aspects of my life.

When you look at money, which is just energy, with fear, you are building a wall around yourself to the ebb and flow of monetary wealth. If you are desperately afraid of losing money, worried about spending money where it needs to be spent (such as on bills) or you are watching the numbers in your account with obsession, I can assure you, it will continuously feel as though there is absolutely no movement in the financial abundance facet of your life. And if you do see movement, it will always happen to be a decline and not an incline, because that's what this energy draws to you.

I was so hyper-fixated on how wealth helped define my appearance of success to others, that I could have been making six figures and I still wouldn't have felt secure or satisfied. I was compulsively preoccupied with loving money because I felt that's what successful people do, and I was unable to narrow this down the why.

Don't get me wrong; money isn't bad. It's just energy. And, I assure you, that God wants all people to be financially abundant, but when we direct all our attention to a single source of energy, that offsets the world's energetic balance. Nothing is meant to be worshiped or focused on in absolutes or extremes. If the energy that you are putting out to harness the energy of monetary wealth is one that is rooted in the emotion of fear, then chaos ensues.

COMFORTABLE IS NOT A SYNONYM FOR ABUNDANT

I CORRELATED COMFORT WITH HAPPINESS

The movies I watched, the words I heard from family, the conversations I had with friends, all told me the same thing: each milestone I hit will bring me the lifetime joy that I seek. I truly believed that the car, the house, the steady job, and the comfortable relationship would be what was needed to live a satisfied and complete life. Each milestone checked would be an item off my "to-do" list and a win in the "completed human" category.

You see so many memes on the internet these days about how Millennials are just longing to own a house; they're tired of crazy markets and fed up with renting at exorbitant prices. All of North America feeds young people this idea that the house is what you really need to be complete, and everything that stands in the way of you reaching that goal is the enemy.

I was able to reach that goal. Quite young, may I add. I entered the housing market one week before my 24th birthday in 2012, before there was a huge explosion in both pricing and demand. Not only did I hit that Millennial checkpoint, but I did it way ahead of my peers, on my own. I should have been so joyful and I should have felt so complete at this point!

The fact of the matter is that I had my first mental breakdown on the day I got my keys to that house. I literally fell to the ground in my new driveway and screamed at the top of my lungs. It was a combination of everything else in my life, but also pure frustration with the fact that everyone built this house up to be what I needed to be able to have joy in my life. I had the keys but couldn't find that joy... *where was it hiding?*

I was called crazy - something I won't forget because I realize now that being gaslit in a moment of such a strong cry for help was a heartbreaking response from someone I trusted. Where was the happiness I was promised from purchasing this house? All I saw were the bills adding up, the stress of paperwork in an already busy life and having to clean and manage a home that was way bigger than what I needed. Nevertheless, I needed this house, according to everything I was taught. So why weren't things adding up to the elation I was supposed to feel?

Still, a home meant comfort and security! It meant a milestone reached - one of the big ones! That's meant to be a joyous occasion!

I didn't feel an ounce of it.

I tried to find joy by bragging about my house purchase on social media in order to rake in the external validation in the form of "congratulations" comments, thinking that maybe that would make me feel happy.

So, here I was in my big house, working my 8am to 4pm, Monday to Friday job, in a steady relationship and making enough money to avoid financial struggles. I had the perfect comfortable ingredients to bake a happy mediocre life. Everything I was meant to feel grateful for was adding to the weight of the question looming inside me - is this really what life is all about? *Is this it?*

The problem with comfortable is that you tend to ignore, or sweep under the rug, all the parts of life that seem *off*. You compartmentalize all the aspects of your existence that question how you may have been lied to because you are cozy and secure and *should* be happy.

Change and risk are scary. Not to mention, they take effort. So, it's much better to float around in comfort and convince yourself that the joy you were promised will come soon enough.

Reflecting from where I am in life right now, I feel like this acceptance of comfortable is more of an issue in North America than it is for other Western countries. We are sold comfortable from the moment we start playing house at daycare or we are asked what we want to be when we grow up. We soak it up like a sponge, preparing our own checklist of milestones that we can start working towards, believing happiness is sitting at the end of it all.

Maybe we should start asking children *who* they want to be when they grow up instead of *what* they want to be. When we answer with characteristics we want to develop and skills we want to learn along the way, the path expands for us. It's not linear because things such as "being a good person" are developed in numerous ways and through endless worldly adventures, not by a single milestone.

Yet, milestones are safe and, therefore, milestones are more comfortable. And comfortable should make us happy *enough*. Happy *enough* is more than we deserve and we should be content with what we get, because people have it worse or haven't been able to cross off those checklist items as efficiently as you. So, be happy. Don't be selfish. How could you possibly be depressed with all this? Get over it. Look at your life! You're crazy. You have everything you need.

Comfortable doesn't develop the skills and characteristics that make you a better human. Comfortable is just a false sense of safety in an uncertain world. People are scared to make changes out of comfortable because those items outside the checklist of life do not guarantee the happiness that these milestones are meant to guarantee. They could end up being big disappointments! Disappointment causes discomfort, so it's best to just stay centered in "just okay." "Just okay" is better than all the negative feelings that can come from something not working out as you hoped or expected.

And so, I also stayed in a "just okay" life with a "just okay" relationship for four years. I wasn't really unhappy, but I wasn't happy in this relationship either (but of course my social media followers didn't know about that). I was okay. I was comfortable. It was safe.

Sure, this person broke my trust numerous times in the partnership and, sure, I resented him for moving into my house and not contributing as an adult to the housework and maintenance of the space, but it was fine. Fine is better than alone. Because this is one of those milestones that everyone in life told me I needed to check off my list.

Alone is not a milestone. An incomplete checklist is an incomplete life. An incomplete life means I am incomplete as a functioning, adult human being. I am not complete if I am alone.

Of course, I now know all of this to be a lie.

THE TREND OF UNFULFILLED RELATIONSHIPS

Settling in relationships was a pattern I seemed to repeat frequently. While this relationship that I was in at this moment in my life was "just okay," there were many others that were not acceptable at all, yet I still remained trapped in them.

This trend of dating just to fill the void of emptiness I felt - only to have the void expand with the presence of this "other" - was a challenge to break. I tried to rationalize away the toxic behaviours, and I internalized a lot of external lies about relationships as being *my truths*. This included the age-old lie of, "fighting in relationships is healthy."

Yes, this is an age-old lie. Period.

I will dive deeper into the discovery of this later in my book but I want to tell you now, don't believe a word of it.

No one ever really clarifies what "fighting" means in this sentence. And so, I allowed myself to be emotionally abused, mentally manipulated, and gaslit by so many partners in my life. I stressed my self-worth and spoke highly of myself by bragging about my achievements, but still I continued to let small partners make me feel like absolute garbage.

I know that we should never blame the victim in abusive relationships, but I do blame myself in my particular case. I knew better! I really did know better than to settle for those men that worked, daily, to break me down, which fed the idea of "being alone is incomplete, and being together with them is better than nothing."

I allowed them, and I allowed myself, to be convinced that this was as good as it gets and that sometimes you just need to settle for bad because it could be worse. None of these people deserved me, but I still allowed them to consume every ounce of my mental, emotional, physical, and spiritual energy.

I allowed myself to be:

- Cheated on (emotionally and physically)
- Called stupid and crazy
- Told I am nothing without them (the partner)
- Emotionally manipulated by suicide threats
- Financially used
- Mentally drained dry
- Pushed to the very edge of a complete breakdown
- Groomed

Remember that I use "allowed myself" for *my particular case* because I intuitively knew this wasn't normal and this was wrong, but I continued to return to it. Everything inside me screamed, "run from this," in every case, but I stayed. It's like watching as the rot of a limb spreads when you know you should just cut it off. I knew what I had to do but instead I was watching as the disease took over me. I was watching as each relationship was slowly eating me alive.

I didn't do anything about it because I was severely unhappy, overall. I was lied to about everything else that would bring me joy in life, so how could a relationship be any different?

According to my internal dialogue, it was just another lie on the milestone checklist. However, it was a milestone, nonetheless, so I may as well accept it for what it is - one more step to being a complete, realized, and fully satisfied human!

I continuously returned to toxic relationships because it was easier than healing. Healing is far messier and far more intense than just settling into an unhappy and unhealthy partnership. It doesn't take work to just give up, but it takes work to overcome the root of where it all stems from, and I didn't want to work.

I believe that a lot of these toxic relationships came down to needing external validation.

NEEDING EXTERNAL VALIDATION

I grew up desperately seeking the approval of my parents through my grades in school. I was given the impression that my failure meant their failure, and that responsibility was on my shoulders. I later learned that this is called subjugation.

My parents often told me that my only responsibility in life is school; they wouldn't approve me getting a part-time job when I was in high school or university because they didn't want to distract from my studies. I do appreciate being given this sole focus in life because it did make me have a greater passion for education, but it also meant that I was expected to be the best of the best when it came to my grades.

For me, when showing my results on tests and

assignments, it wasn't about what I learned or where I grew, it was about how happy it would make them. If it was 98%, it should have been 100. If it was average, it wasn't good enough. Don't even get me started on any mark lower than 80%! My grades gave me severe anxiety, but I don't think I ever expressed this to my parents who just wanted me to succeed in life.

Thus, my foundation of needing the external validation of others was established, and my people-pleasing personality - which had me going time and time again to men who didn't deserve my attention in young adulthood - had a place to rest upon.

My successes in life were not about me. My parents wanted what they believed was the best for me and my success as an adult in this world, but I didn't really know what *I* wanted. The milestones I was chasing and the checklists I was completing were not for me in any way, shape, or form. They were used to make other people proud of me. They were shown off as badges of honour so that people could tell me how good I was, how smart I was, how hard-working I was, etc., and so my parents had bragging rights for their friends and for family. I didn't really know, or understand, how to do something *just for me,* because I was continuously made to believe that pursuing what makes *just me* happy was selfish, and that wasn't how life worked.

The pursuit of external validation for internal serenity

is obviously a chase that is done in vain. It never leads to happiness because you correlate other people's opinions as validation points for your joy, and you become incapable of finding the joy of life without it. It's what makes people addicted to social media and to celebrity-like recognition and approval from others. It's what can lead people to eating disorders and identity-based issues. It's also what kept me in a career that stopped bringing me joy and spiritual satisfaction, just a few years in.

I BELIEVED CAREER PATHS WERE LINEAR

These milestones that I was checking off followed a very meticulous and linear pattern: complete school with high grades, get into a university undergraduate program and graduate at the top of the class, enter into teacher's college, get a job before my colleagues, stay in the system until I retire with a comfortable teacher's pension…

In Canada, teaching is a pretty honourable job. So much so, that the competition while I was in the program was fierce. We were warned in our classes to, "expect to be unemployed for a few years following graduation" - something my parents immediately said I could not make excuses for.

Teaching in Ontario not only gives you a secure, unionized job with incredible pay, but you also have an excellent insurance and pension program that begins on your first day of work.

In my dad's words, I was, "set for life," so how could I even *consider* leaving such a career? Why would I even think of starting over and losing all that security, *right?* Where could it possibly lead to except to higher positions within education? Since milestones and checklists mean you are never truly happy and always looking for the "next best thing," it's only logical that, in regards to my career, it would proceed in the same manner but up the educational ladder.

If I wasn't finding the emotional and spiritual satisfaction in Classroom A, it must be waiting for me in Classroom B. If Classroom B manifested a mental breakdown that lead to another round of severe depression and anxiety, it must be Position C that had joy waiting for me. The path was straight and the safety of the profession was set, so I was told by my parents, friends, and colleagues to not stray and to stay on course.

People who enter education are naturally *nurturers* and those in compassionate careers, much like healthcare, carry the same mentality that I grew up with: we have a responsibility to others, this job is safe and long-term, we will be comfortable... so stick to it. Too soft and eager to please everyone else, we keep to the grind, even as it slowly breaks us down and destroys us, bit by bit. So many people are now *talking* about teachers leaving education, but who is actually doing it? We can't. We are trapped by our learned guilt and desire to please others.

I realized that it was not possible for me to be in a role that required strict monitoring of my identity. When you become a teacher, you do not turn off the educator cap when you leave the school grounds. You wear that hat everywhere you go and you are defined as "Teacher" first and "Claudia" second. And, as such, everything you do is monitored under this lens of judgment.

"You can't do that, you're a teacher."

"You can't say that, you're a teacher."

"You can't share your personal life with students, you'll get written up."

"You cannot talk about those difficult topics in your classroom, you'll get in trouble."

All I wanted was to be authentically me without apologizing for it, but, as an educator, that's not allowed. Imagine working under a job title for 24 hours a day, seven days a week… that's what being a teacher felt like. And I certainly wasn't paid enough to do this every hour of every day for the rest of my life.

The educational system wanted me to create obedient little robots and nothing felt right about that. Success was measured by test scores, academic awards, and graduations. I wanted to create joyful, creative, expressive, and wise young learners who were ready to grow up in an increasingly challenging world. I wanted them to be radically joyful about the life *they were choosing for themselves* because I was increasingly depressed by the life I let others define for me. They didn't deserve that and I wanted them to know that they had a choice to design the life they wanted.

All my colleagues used to tell me that it gets better the longer you teach, and that they were all very satisfied with the career path they chose. These same people dreaded Mondays and celebrated Fridays. They looked drained and broken during testing season or report card writing periods. They lived routine lives with no excitement, living in a typical Canadian city, living a work-focused Canadian life. They didn't seem undeniably happy and they didn't appear to be living their *dream life*. They were just settling into the comfort of the routine, and I felt myself getting there too.

That terrified me.

When I saw my colleagues receive their ten, twenty, and even thirty years of service certificates from the board office, my anxiety skyrocketed. I couldn't imagine myself doing this for another five years, let alone thirty. The thought of doing that every Monday to Friday until I turned 60 and retired made me want to scream.

Surely this couldn't be what life was about? Is this really where it stops - you get the job and you stay there until you make enough money to retire? This can't be it!

Not only were the routines and the expectations dreadfully awful, but the damage this job did to me *as a person* was immense. Rude and entitled parents spiritually, and emotionally, broke me down. Competitive and gossipy colleagues mentally drained me. The go-go-go routine of the day was extorting me, physically. Everyone seemed to hate teachers, criticize teachers, and have comments about the job without ever having stepped foot in it. Day by day, I was falling apart. My empath self just couldn't handle all this negativity, hate, and energy of judgment that was continuously flowing my way.

POOR AND PERFORMATIVE SPIRITUAL PRACTICE

The primary reason that made me unable to handle the negative energy directed towards me during my career as an educator boiled down to a poor spiritual practice.

As I mentioned, I have always been "in-tune," even as a child. I could sense things, see things, and I had predictive dreams. At a certain point, my fear with what I was seeing, hearing, and knowing caused me to turn off my gifts. This was primarily triggered by the eye rolls and doubt projected onto me by adults. From the age of twelve onwards, I used Tarot cards consistently (a life-changing gift from my mother during a bookshop visit) and was always drawn to mythical stories and histories.

Unfortunately, as a young adult trying to re-establish her spiritual identity, when you are as undeniably unhappy as I was, you will grab onto and buy the first thing that promises you spiritual happiness the quickest. Social media spaces are filled with this fake spirituality.

Light and love are the quick fixes to all of life's problems. Manifesting through the Law of Attraction will get you everything you want (not need) to be happy, and if you don't get it, you're not thinking about it hard enough. The ego is meant to be embraced and power is desirable. All these things and more, I ate them up.

Why wouldn't I turn to a spirituality that promised me happiness quickly, and power in the process?

The spirituality I was buying into told me:

- There's nothing wrong with you, there's only something wrong with everyone and everything around you.
- You need to rise above and focus solely on developing your third eye. That is how you become truly gifted.
- Buy this crystal to be happy. Use this sage to be happy. Read this book to be happy. You aren't cool enough in the spiritual community

THE TRANSFORMATIONAL PATH

if you don't use these cards. You aren't cool if you don't follow this spiritual teacher.
- Materialism doesn't contradict with spirituality, don't worry. You *need* these things to be happy.
- If you're not learning about each and every spiritual practice, you're not wise enough.
- Your intuition is the same as your emotions, so your emotional reactions are spiritual in nature. If you are mad, get really mad and let people know it!
- Anyone who doesn't have the same mindset or beliefs as you isn't as wise or spiritually developed as you.
- Fame and fortune are what awaits you when you are truly spiritually prosperous. Rock that #GirlBoss in your social media profile. Hustle until you die! Love and Light solve every problem and anyone who says otherwise isn't Loving and Lighting hard enough.
- Become so spiritually gifted that other people feel they *need* you in order to survive on this earthly plane.

This spirituality I was developing turned me into an ego-driven individual, and an angry one at that. None of the practices I was digesting brought me the joy that I was promised, and, like my milestones, I was consistently searching for it in the next best thing being sold to me. I truly felt wiser and spiritually better than everyone because of everything I was reading, practicing, and consuming.

This actually led me down a path of social activism. When social activism is being pursued from an, "I'm better and wiser than you," mentality, it's really just anger and trauma being projected at others because you don't want to deal with it yourself. And so, I thought that anyone who thought differently than me, anyone who said something that triggered and caused an emotional reaction in me, and anyone who held religious beliefs that strayed from the "Love and Light" of my spiritual path was trash. They deserved to be spoken to like the trash they are. They needed to be torn apart until they thought and acted exactly like me. How ironic, considering I was preaching Love and Light, *right?*

This is what spirituality that is rooted in ego will do to a person. It makes you angry and has you hyper-focusing on the differences between us, rather than the core that unites all of us: the God energy that flows through everyone. This path of spirituality pits you against one another instead of having you focus on self-development and personal growth. It has you competing for "spiritual milestones" instead of bringing you a place of centered calm and understanding. It is rooted in division and superiority, not in unity and oneness with the Universe.

This path of spirituality that I fell into was very performative; like a theatre show to the masses to prove how "super spiritual" you are. The more angry, intense, and demanding of respect you were, the more powerful you were in that space. The more you bought, owned, and showed off, the more respected you would be by others for "manifesting it all."

This ego path that tells you nothing is wrong with you, you're perfect as you are and everyone else needs fixing, buries all of your shadows under the label of "Love and Light." It is a path that doesn't actually encourage healing of traumas, past life regression to solve present day issues and understanding and overcoming of karmic debts; there is no actual restorative growth happening. There is no real healing, at all.

It's really about burying it with a smile, or buying things like crystals and oracle cards until you think you can't feel it anymore, and that's the end of it. At the same time, it has you believing you're wise enough to lead and teach others! Ego-ruled chaos leading the blind - can you imagine how dangerous that is?

It makes sense that nothing in my life was Zen and nothing seemed to bring me joy when the very foundation of my being - my spirituality - was such a damn mess.

THE WRONG DEFINITION OF MANIFESTATION AND TRUTH

This crumbled foundation of spirituality caused a deep misunderstanding of Truth and a skewed definition of manifestation. In fact, the word *manifest* still triggers me a bit because of how it is sold in spiritual communities.

According to the majority of the celebrity gurus out there, manifesting is:

- Whatever I want in life can be mine! All I need to do is think about it really hard, or write it down 55 times. Or, 33 times for 3 days. If one doesn't work, try the other.
- If I'm not getting what I want, I'm not thinking about it hard enough. I'm not making powerful enough affirmations and I'm not meditating on it with enough spiritual force.
- The Law of Attraction will only work for people who put sticky notes on their mirror about what they want.

If you're reading these points and thinking how absolutely stupid they sound, you're right. Nevertheless, take a deeper dive into the books you are reading on manifestation and you'll find a similar message there, wrapped in a different jargon. *All you need to have what you want is to think about it, always, and it will come to you!*

It's complete nonsense.

Basically, manifestation was sold to me as a "sit back and watch it fall into your lap" magic spell that people who are spiritually gifted are blessed with. What this causes is an entire group of sad individuals to say, "I suck at manifesting!" or, "I don't believe in manifesting because it never seems to work for me."

I was one of those sad individuals.

That is absolutely *not* what manifestation is, and that's not how it works. If you are expecting all the joys of life to drop into your lap without first putting in the work, then you've completely misunderstood how manifestation functions, just like I did.

The word 'manifest' comes from the Latin etymological root of 'manus' meaning *hand* and 'festus' meaning *attack*. It can be loosely translated or interpreted as, *caught by the hand*. This goes to emphasize that manifestation isn't about sitting back and waiting for something to just happen to you, but that you need to go after what you want and *grab it*. So, why did all these books lie to me?

Instead of holding the quartz crystal in your left hand and saying what you want three times under a new moon, manifestation is about planning. You begin with an intention or goal; this is what many would call a mantra or "manifestation focus", but not clarifying that it is a goal makes it less tangible and attainable. This intention directs your purpose. The next steps are completely up to you.

Another misunderstanding about manifestation that I allowed to influence my spirituality was that it works at the snap of your fingers. Sorry to be the bearer of bad news, but God isn't a magic genie who grants your wishes and God certainly doesn't work on your time. Just because *you* think you're ready and deserve this to happen to you doesn't mean you are, *spiritually speaking*.

Manifestation is a process that requires extensive lesson learning and patience, and the Universe always provides for you, exactly when you are ready. At the time, I didn't realize that. Instead, I began to resent God and the Universe when my happiness wasn't going up, despite the number in my bank account going down as I bought the crystal, the sage, the new moon water, the magic spell book, and the guru's workbook on manifestation, just like I was told.

Why wasn't manifestation working for me? Why wasn't I seeing the joy and abundance I was promised?

The problem this all came down to was a misunderstanding of Truth.

Yes, that is Truth with a capital T - that's an important distinction. I really believed that the influencer life coaches and gurus I was following on social media were feeding me Truth, and that spiritual ascension was rooted in:

- Feeding my emotional pleasures; if it made me unhappy, it was bad - likewise, if it made me feel good, it was spiritual
- Material focus for spiritual gain; buy the items to show others how spiritual you truly are
- Power and fame as a reflection of your spiritual skills; if you don't have a massive following, you aren't having a massive impact
- Doing it all; the only way to prove you're wise and knowledgeable is to dip your toes in a little bit of everything

However, real Truth, the kind that makes a solid foundation upon which to build your spiritual life, is nothing like that.

Truth, with a capital T, is Universe-al, it's God-centered, and it's Divine in nature. It doesn't change from one day to the next, it doesn't require materialism to be satiated, and it is not emotional.

I was being sold the idea that Truth was all about my emotional reactions to reality and that everything I was projecting was valid. I know this now to be defined as a trigger. An emotionally triggered reaction to reality is not authentic Truth.

Truth is meant to make you feel calm, centered, and at peace with the world. What I was being sold made me feel angry with the world, judgmental, continuously looking for opportunities to "cancel" others in order to step on their backs and rise up the spirituality ladder, and had me performing to impress others. There is nothing constant or reliable about that spirituality, so it makes sense that the house I built upon that foundation was completely weak and fragile.

What really stood out about the spirituality I was embracing, was the fact that it didn't really talk about healing what is involved with the tough process of healing. It frequently mentioned, "embracing your ego and your shadows as your friend" which is actually a disaster waiting to happen.

It said, "healing is necessary," but then stopped right there. It seemed to push the idea that meditation could whisk away your traumas and that the right crystals could cure all anxieties. It suggested micro-dosing and drinking ceremonial grade cacao to spiritually awaken oneself and transcend triggers. It provided quick band-aids to cover up the mess inside, but never really provided a solution to sweep it all away.

What I eventually realized is, that without that healing, I really couldn't expect to reach the mountain peak of joy that I was so desperately seeking. Without truly analyzing what patterns in my life I was repeating, what toxic relationships I was allowing myself to be immersed in and what true mental and emotional issues needed addressing, I would continue in a circle of despair. I would continue to be misguided by what I thought was Truth but was merely ego, and I would continue to blame it on not being able to *manifest* well enough.

I BURIED MY DARKNESS

One of the things I liked the most about the spirituality and truth that I was sold, was that it didn't actually take any work at all. I could just write something down and it was supposed to come to me. I could hold the right crystal and drink the right full moon water and all my problems would be solved. I didn't really need to put in any work into *actually* healing. Except, at the same time, I wasn't actually seeing results, and I couldn't quite narrow down why (even though it was so very obvious).

I buried my darkness because I thought I could

"spirituality-it" away with the right tools, mantras, and by reading the right texts. I devoured books that told me how awesome I was and how no one else knew it; there was nothing about me that needed changing. I ate up the victim mentality that this spirituality was feeding me and I called it empowerment. In the famous words of Maury Pauvich from the 90s, "That was a lie."

These lies and avoidance made it impossible for me to actually handle stress and had me continuing patterns that never brought about the change I was looking for. There were aspects of my behaviour that were toxic and unfair to others, but I believed that they just needed to deal with it. The way I handled stress was through complete breakdowns and panic attacks.

I looked for short-term solutions to my issues because it was simpler for me. After all, I was being told that spiritual growth was easy, so why wouldn't I look for a band-aid to cover the mess hiding below?

This avoidance also brought with it a severe addiction to social media, because the approval I gained and the instant gratification that I had from likes, comments, and DMs from strangers added to the, "I'm perfect as I am," mentality that I was eating away at.

Avoidance, burial, or ego-feeding was way easier than actually healing.

Healing is messy, it's painful, it takes risk, and unlearning. It requires a careful self-assessment and an honesty that you've, likely, never been told to have with yourself before. The books that tell you how badass and great you are, forget to mention the most important thing: you're only badass and great after you actually do the healing. That can't be skipped. In fact, it's the very first step to truly being able to manifest what you need in your life.

Popular spirituality glorifies the *third eye* - the energy center that connects you with "seeing" through the veil, heightening your intuition, and Awakening.

They forget that an over-active Chakra is just as dangerous as one that's blocked, and that the flow of energy needs to pass through all your energy centers smoothly in order for you to be complete, whole, and healed. This modern spirituality abandons the root Chakra which is, quite literally, central to keeping you *rooted*, humble, and balanced, overall.

The social media and influencer spirituality worships ascension and forgets that we have come into these particular bodies for good reason: to learn specific lessons, to live in this incarnation fully and completely, and to use the relationships we have to break karmic and generational ties.

We can't just ignore it!

We can't just bury all of our problems away and pray that life will be awesome, despite it. We can't take the drug to escape our body and Ascend. We can't expect everyone else to change, to stop projecting their darkness onto us, and to stop suffocating our awesome if we aren't willing to also do the same for others. We can't simply assume that everyone else has healing to do but we don't also have to do the work.

It's illogical, impractical, and a false, ego-based spirituality. It will never bring you the joy you seek.

It took me a while to realize this.

"I can't stand to think my life is going so fast and I'm not really living it."

- *Ernest Hemingway*

CHAPTER TWO
WHAT ACCEPTANCE LOOKS LIKE

Among all these layers of depression, anxiety, and general unhappiness, I was hiding a dream.

In 2010, I went to Paris, France, for the very first time. I was reluctant to do a stopover there because, as I stressed to my partner at the time, nothing about it interested me; I didn't like Parisians and France didn't excite me. I guess the Universe likes to teach you lessons on humility because within 20 minutes of being in Paris, something felt… *different*.

I was blessed to have the opportunity to travel a lot as a child with my family. My parents weren't rich by any means, but their one goal was to save for a family vacation every year. I had seen a lot of the world by the time I was 22 (2010), including many visits to my ancestral home in Italy, however, something about Paris felt like nothing before it. *It felt like home.*

This was the first time in my life where I found a place that felt like home. Even the life I established for myself in Canada didn't feel right, comfortable, or safe the way Paris did. This city felt like the be-all and the end-all to my complete existence.

Paris called to me in every bookstore, where I devoured books by ex-pats who gave up their unfulfilling American lives to pursue a dream, drowning in cheese, and baguettes. Paris called to me at antique markets where old, white iron items made me think of summers in Provence. Paris called to me with films like *Amelie* and *Midnight in Paris*. Paris called to me through the books of my favourite authors, the American writers of the 1920s, who built a life for themselves in her streets.

I wanted that life. I wanted to live in those streets. I wanted to write in those cafes.

For as long as I can remember, I have been writing books, stories, poetry, and more, to share with family and friends. Writing was always an innate part of my being and, even as a child, I found every excuse to put pencil to paper and start crafting magic. Wanting to be a professional writer didn't feel like a pipe dream to me

WHAT ACCEPTANCE LOOKS LIKE

but like a part of my life purpose. I didn't really know *what* I was meant to create and release into the world, but I knew I was meant to create *something*.

Encouraged by my favourite writer Ernest Hemingway who famously spoke the words, "If you are lucky enough to have lived in Paris as a young [wo]man, then wherever you go for the rest of your life, it stays with you, for Paris is a moveable feast," I knew where I was meant to manifest this piece of myself - in Paris. The calling was too strong to ignore.

For the first time in my life, I had a bucket list item, a milestone, a goal, that was fully and completely mine. *I* wanted it. No one else wanted it for me; just me, with all of my soul and being. I longed for it as a woman longs for her long-distance lover. It was truly and completely all I desired with every fiber of my being. And this longing never ceased. This dream of calling myself *Parisienne* saturated every aspect of my life, while simultaneously reminding me how unsatisfied I was with the role I was playing in Ontario, where I felt like a visitor and an alien.

I agonized for Paris. I wrote about her in my journals with such yearning and hunger that you could *feel* the pain in my words. Unfortunately, a life in Paris didn't fit with the linear goals and secure Canadian life everyone else had planned out for me. And so, the anxiety that manifested at the fear of Paris never becoming my reality, mounted and even broke my internal dam at various points in my life. I was overwhelmed with the feeling of, "I'm stuck here and there is simply nothing I can do about it."

In September 2016, I wrote these words in my journal:

> "Am I wasting time agonizing for Paris from thousands of miles away?
>
> I don't want to regret my life, just because I let moments and opportunities pass me. I don't want to miss those chances to maybe do something really great. I want every moment to count and I want to try my hand at everything I can. I'm a dreamer, after all.
>
> And so, why do I wait for Paris? Why do I slowly let this opportunity pass me by, and risk that I might reach a moment where the dream isn't available to me anymore?
>
> Asking myself these questions makes me really upset, and also makes me feel a little less confident. I pride myself in being impulsive (it's allowed for some amazing things to happen in my life), but what holds back the impulse this time around?

WHAT ACCEPTANCE LOOKS LIKE

> What am I afraid of?
> I feel uninspired. I feel unsatisfied and unfulfilled. I'll be 29 in a few months, and although I've achieved a lot for myself and by myself in a short amount of time, I don't feel fully and completely happy. I keep searching for more. Paris plays a big part in that "more".
> I continue to dream about my move, and wonder when I'll simply take the leap and make it my reality."

Unfortunately, I would continue to wait and dream a little longer because, as I now realize, God doesn't work on my time. Instead, the Universe always has a plan. Working on a rushed schedule hinders your inner growth and development; it's like playing a Chopin symphony at three times the speed - it's just not right. By trying to speed up the process, you're basically telling God, "Listen, I don't trust what you've got planned and I'm doing this my way," and yet clearly *my way* wasn't bringing me the joy I so desired.

TIMELINES AND EXPECTATIONS

I spent all of my life developing my existence around set and expected milestones that coincided with precise, age-based timelines. I was slowly beginning to learn that that's not actually how the Universe works. The idea behind expectations, and getting hooked on when (and how) you want this to happen for you, comes from a place of ego and control. I was viewing delays or setbacks as debilitating roadblocks that I couldn't possibly overcome, and I let those challenges add to my overall depression.

In December 2016, just a few months after that agonizing journal entry, I went to sign my mortgage renewal on my house. It felt like the ultimate trap; locked into an Ontario house that brought me no joy for another five years. To me, I believed this was yet another signifier that Paris was not meant to be. I cried in my car after leaving the bank - the opposite of how many people feel when they get a mortgage approval, I'm sure.

I wrote this in my journal:

"Have I just resigned myself to the fate of the comfortable and reliable? Did I just settle? Did I just sign away my dreams? I had goals of making Paris my home in my 30th year… I'll be 29 in February. Now what? Do my "goals" and "dreams" really have a purpose? Are they just fairy tales?

WHAT ACCEPTANCE LOOKS LIKE

I can't say I returned home excited by my lowered interest rate and lowered monthly mortgage payments (yes, these things do excite adults) because it was overshadowed by the loss of years I could have been in Paris. It was clouded by the idea of four more years in a place where I am not truly happy, fulfilled, or inspired.

People say, "Make the best of the time you have and stop dreaming of the future", "Make your home into a place you want to be" etc. Don't get me wrong, my house is awesome. I am constantly moving around the space to suit my needs and making it more wonderful to be immersed in. There are nerdy things everywhere you look. It's a house full of life and fun. But it's a house on an urban street in an urban city in the Greater Toronto Area [built upon] the Western mentality of, "work until you die". I can't do it. It's eating away at my soul.

And yet, I've resigned myself to another four years of it. What have I done?"

I have now learned that one of the keys to successful manifestation is understanding the importance of time. Time, delays, challenges, and roadblocks are not there just to frustrate you or make you fall into a greater disappointment with the Universe. They are always there to teach you something and, more often than not, it's something that takes many months or many years to unravel.

I find that the more you obsess over God working things out on your own timeline, the more you'll be disappointed because, quite simply put, it won't happen that way. It never happens that way.

If you're incapable of letting go of expectations or releasing the requirement of having dreams play out according to the years you've mentally set for them ("I want to be married by 28, I want a child by 32, I want the CEO position by 35" or, in my case, "I want to be in Paris by 30"), you will actually find that you encounter far more stop signs along your journey. And it's no coincidence either.

I was so overwhelmed by the numbers ("I am turning 29 and I set my goals for 30!") that I didn't take a moment to realize that: 1. A year is actually a very long time to have something come to fruition, and 2. I was in no way ready at the time of writing that journal entry to begin my soul-journey in Paris.

HEAVY HEALING

When I was 18 years old, I was sexually assaulted by a person I considered to be a friend. That was not only my first sexual experience, but it was also how I started my journey in University because it happened just a few months after beginning this independent stage of my life.

My entire youth was clean, party-free, and kept under a pretty strict upbringing, and now my very first taste of freedom included sexual assault. Is this what happens when you don't follow the rules and regulations of others? When you live an independent life, not dictated by what others expect of you and have planned for you, do you simultaneously experience trust-destroying physical trauma? This is, of course, the connection my brain (and spirit) made.

I didn't want to face the reality of what had happened to me and this mentality of "going against the plan" made me feel embarrassed, ashamed, and disgusted in myself. I would preface talking about it with, "I *think* I was raped," and when I asked the person about it, I remember saying, "Did you *try to have sex with me, last night?"* (That wasn't sex; sex is consensual. There was absolutely nothing I consented to in my blacked out stupor of that night.)

I believed that if I never talked about it, it would disappear. This is what happens when you don't stick to

THE TRANSFORMATIONAL PATH

the plan and now I must ignore it and get myself back on the track that people had set for me. I was learning through the spiritual gurus who I followed on social media that, if I meditated deep enough, it would heal itself, and vanish into the abyss. Influencer spirituality often shames people who rely on "real doctors" alongside their spiritual healing, and I believed it. I believed that the cards, crystals, and affirmations should be enough to heal this trauma.

For six years, I buried and I denied that part of my lived experience until, one day, I learned the harsh lesson of compartmentalizing: the more you shove pain into the crevices of your being, the bigger the explosion at the end of it all. I had a hell of an explosion when a nonchalant rape joke triggered my many years of denial.

When you bury trauma, you build a foundation of your identity upon sand. Ignoring the darkness doesn't mean it ceases to exist, it just means that it's hiding under the surface, ready to show its face when you are least prepared to handle it. When my trauma was triggered and it emerged, it came raging, ready to take me with it. My medically diagnosed depression and anxiety were amplified beyond control, and I was also being diagnosed with Post Traumatic Stress Disorder (PTSD) on top of it all - the trifecta of mental instability!

One morning, I woke up with the realization that I *had been* sexually assaulted, that this event completely altered the entire trajectory of my life, and that wasn't okay. As the dam broke and my emotions flooded me, I sat in front of my laptop and composed a message to the Police Chief of my city. I didn't know what else to do or how else to go about raising a report for something like this, that happened to me eight years ago. I didn't even have intentions set with how I wanted this to unfold. I just knew, in that moment, that this was the release I needed. So, I responded to that pain accordingly.

Eventually, my email to the Police Chief culminated in a formal report and deciding to face my former friend in court. Now, a little background behind this decision is needed to emphasize how the cards were already stacked against me before this even began; my assailant's dad was once the head judge of the region I lived in, and his two siblings were lawyers. Despite knowing this, I made the decision to take him to court for a few important reasons:

1. I was satisfied by the idea that the mere fear of conviction that would overwhelm this boy, could potentially trigger a request for forgiveness from the Universe (releasing our karmic ties) as well as scare him out of hurting anyone, ever again.
2. I realized that both my voice and my story had power and value and I was worth being

listened to as he was forced to look me in the eye.
3. I recognized the strength in reversing the narrative alone, of me as a victim and him in power - a dynamic which switches in a courtroom and returns the energetic balance, regardless of the outcome.

Unfortunately, after a year of waiting for a court date and a month of torture in the court system, he was acquitted by the judge working the case due based on insufficient proof to make him guilty beyond a reasonable doubt.

Although, I didn't need a guilty verdict to heal - something inside me had already begun to shift and I said to myself, "I forgive him, fully and completely, for what he has done to me."

Riding on the waves of that forgiveness energy, I started a new therapy called EMDR (Eye Movement Desensitisation and Reprocessing).

I would like to begin by saying that therapy is worth every penny of investment. Spirituality is essential to a well-lived life, but therapy is there to help you heal human trauma efficiently. Being Canadian and having gone through the court system, thankfully, the cost of my therapy was covered by the government. Nonetheless, I truly believe that it's worth taking out a loan to cover the cost of quality therapy. It allows you to completely restructure the foundation of your life while simultaneously eliminating what no longer serves you, releasing it with energetic neutrality so that karmic ties are cut and triggers cease to have a hold over you.

Triggers are essentially emotional reactions to your *perceived* reality. They happen when you are projecting and are incapable of managing or releasing your fear and pain. I used to believe that the world had to cater to make me feel more comfortable with my PTSD triggers, eliminating them *for me* so I didn't have to do the work myself, but therapy taught me the truth; I needed to learn to completely own and dominate my triggers so that they no longer built my reality for me. I realized I could not change or control how people acted, what they said, or how they treated me. I could only ever control how I responded to it.

This was life-changing.

Influencer and social media spirituality also tells you that the world has to change *for you* and that your emotional reactions are valid and normal and should be catered to. It tells you that you're awesome the way you are and that you need to stop doubting it and just live unapologetically. However, living with this state of reaction that you cannot turn off and projected fear is not normal and is, in fact, pretty selfish to force people to accept.

When you are energetically balanced and aligned with the Universe's energy, you are essentially neutral and Zen; it's the reason why so many Buddhists strive for Nirvana. They don't go searching for emotionally triggered reactions, anger, fear, and chaos! Who would want to infinitely be stuck in that state? There is nothing normal about it. While you are worthy and valid, even if you are suffering and triggered, it is unfair to ask others to come out of their stable and centered state to cater to your energetic abnormality.

Therapy allows you to look at your triggers with an objective lens and ultimately decide that you will not allow your emotions and your fear to build your reality for you, and that you are the master of your emotions - they do not control you. This is an extremely hard lesson in healing to learn and most people would rather skip it entirely! It's so much easier to let the wild horse reign free than to take the slow and painful time to train him; training the horse takes *a lot* of work that people would rather avoid (or they would rather have the horse pre-trained for them).

EMDR therapy uses rapid eye movements to basically reprogram traumatic memories in your brain and replace them with a memory of a safe space. The safe space that I developed with my therapist was a cafe on a corner in Paris, overlooking the Notre Dame, with the smell of coffee and baguettes and the sound of bells ringing. If Paris's only purpose was to save my life as a safe space through this therapy process, it had succeeded. I am forever grateful that Paris exists, for this reason alone.

EMDR helped turn every traumatic memory in my life from a vivid image that emotionally impacted me on the daily to a pixelated movie scene happening to someone I didn't recognize as me. It was literal magic. Meditation alone wouldn't have *ever* had the same impact on my personal healing.

UNLEARNING MY OWN TOXIC BEHAVIOUR

My PTSD not only explained my anger, my longing for "quick fixes" and my emotional reactions to the reality I was constructing around me, but it also explained many of my own toxic traits and patterns that I was repeating in my life. When I was able to assess and eliminate my traumatic moments, I was able to eliminate the repetition of those behaviours onto others in my personal life and relationships. I learned how generational trauma worked through my EMDR therapy and healing; when wrong is done to you, you pass those characteristics on to others, unknowingly, because it's how you learn to navigate the world.

I stopped projecting my expectations onto others about how they should live their life and I stopped attributing success to standard milestone achievements. I stopped judging people who pursued happiness over the perfect degree, the perfect job, and the cookie cutter definition of what achievement should look like. I stopped worrying about how other people were living - and their opinion of the life I was creating for myself - and started focusing more intently on my joys. This also meant that I wasn't getting as angry or "triggered" by people with differing opinions, ideas, and political positions.

Healing my PTSD helped me realize that I was *allowing* myself to have emotional reactions to people and to the projected reality around me and, instead of wanting to deal with these issues myself, I wanted other people to do the work for me. If they just removed their opinion/idea/political stance, I'd feel better. This was laziness and is comparable to sweeping trauma under a rug and hoping no one ever looks underneath.

I learned that you cannot remove triggers; you cannot construct a false reality and expect the world to be a safe space. You can only work towards removing how you react to them.

I believed that the people who had these original ideas that made me angry were harmful to my existence, but harmful and triggering are not synonyms. Triggering activates emotional responses in a person, while harmful is actually causing damage to a person's existence. No one was actively damaging me or harming me by existing; no one was actually interfering with my ability to live a normal life by having ideas that differed from my own. I had a choice to respond to my trigger how I wanted to, but I never had the power to expect people to live or think how I wanted them to - this was a toxic response to my trauma and was, in fact, a repetition of behaviour I learned through my traumatic experience. I was passing on my trauma to others, to strangers, and disguising it as social justice and being *woke*.

My healing through therapy helped me to understand that, through my emotional reactions to these triggers, I was allowing my trauma to control my life over and over again. Every time I allowed an emotional response to drive my behaviour, words, and actions, I was giving it power and authority over my being. Reactivity - that Influencer spirituality (as I call it) was telling me was normal and should be embraced - was allowing me to manufacture my truth and ignore Truth, with a capital T. My emotional reaction was not tangible and was not factual, and trying to impose my feelings and reactions on others as Truth was not fair. It could, in fact, have created a new cycle of trauma in their own lives.

I was using my trauma as justification for how I was processing my experience, called Life, and when I was holding onto trauma, I was not healing the emotional processing of this experience. I held onto my feelings towards the world as Truth, and control, when I was in fact being deceived. Emotional reactions are the least reliable foundation upon which to build your cause and your reality.

Rationality, calm, strength, and a careful processing of factual information - not manufactured narratives based on my anger and my sadness - were the real ways to Truth. My emotional reactions made me a judgmental bully, made me passive aggressive, and made me angry at the world. None of these feelings bring about healing, only the distribution of my pain and trauma, which is unfair and cruel.

Instead of quick reactions, I began to ask myself:

- Will my emotional reaction lead to my healing or add to my anger?
- Will my emotional reaction feed the reality I am painting in my mind or add facts to Truth?
- Am I aware that my emotional reaction will not, and cannot, alter the reality that someone else has created for themselves?
- Will this lead to peace or cause more division?
- Am I educating or just trying to force someone to think and act as I deem to be appropriate?

- What difference will my anger-filled reaction truly make in my life or the lives of others?
- What if this energy was spent on healing instead? Will the world go on if I simply move on, ignore, and heal from the trauma that caused this triggered reaction?

Careful reflection usually leads to me walking away from the situation and letting people live their lives in peace, no matter how different their ideas might be from my own and no matter how much I disagree with them. I no longer contribute to expanding the divide through anger and through "canceling" others and instead focus on opportunities where I can bridge the divide, unite spirits, and recognize the light and learning that can come from difference.

Therapy also helped break the cycle of unhealthy relationships that I was continuously drawn into.

HERO SYNDROME

Being a clairaudient, empathetic, and compassionately spiritual person meant that I naturally wanted to fix everything and everyone around me, including the people that I entered into relationships with. However, taking time to properly heal my spiritual injuries through medically sound therapy meant that I was able to look at my relationships through a more objective lens. I learned that I cannot save anyone else before saving myself.

I was entering into relationships with broken people who were desperately looking outside themselves for others to solve their problems for them. They, too, didn't want to do the work. They, too, projected and blamed all their faults and brokenness on everyone and everything outside of themselves, instead of healing and becoming better people.

I dated people who saw the world as the enemy trying to bring them down and I dated people who gaslit me into believing I was the enemy trying to bring them down. They never took responsibility for their words, their behaviours, or their lack of action in their own lives. Nothing was ever by their own hand, no failure ever their own causation. They coddled their trauma as though it was a warm, soothing blanket, and stomped their feet or sulked when life didn't go their way.

If I did meet someone who had a sound handle on their trauma and was making the effort to become a better human being who took sole responsibility for their life and their joy, I quickly turned the other way. Energetically, we didn't line up because I wasn't there yet. So, I fell back into toxic patterns with shattered people who hopelessly wanted me to be broken with them.

I learned to forgive these broken people who used me

as a way to bury their own trauma, because only hard and time-consuming healing allows you to understand the damage an unhealed spirit can do to others. I stopped playing the victim when I recognized that these people were mirrors of my own damage that I needed to uncover, unravel, and make better.

DIVINE TIMING

So, there I was, longing for Paris and crying as I desperately asked the Universe to make all my dreams come true and get me out of here (Ontario), not realizing that there was a plan in order. If I had gone to Paris without having done all that healing, understanding, and realization about life and relationships, I would have repeated many of my same toxic traits and behaviours, only in a new country and paired with all the stresses that come with unfamiliarity.

I thought these setbacks and delays were frustrating, only realizing later that they were *so necessary.* God didn't just magically make Paris happen at the snap of my fingers, or after writing down an affirmation 33 times in a journal, because there was so much still to learn about forgiveness, about my own negative characteristics and about the way the world and Truth work.

My court case didn't succeed because that was not where my growth was meant to happen; I was meant to work at it through my therapy. If I had won my court case, it may have been another instance of me burying the true healing I needed to go through, with a false feeling of accomplishment. I would have said, "I won, and now it is done!" and the deep, painful transformations I went through may never have existed. Not much would have changed in my life and I likely wouldn't have had forgiveness for my assailant, which was a crucial thing I needed to learn. The momentary joy of that win might have turned me away from therapy, only to have my PTSD, depression, and anxiety resurface at a later date.

My therapy allowed me to identify and acknowledge many toxic traits in myself and in others, enabling my growth and betterment. What I, at the time, saw as time passing by without Parisian streets at my feet, the Universe recognized as the rebuilding of the foundation of my authentic self so I was better prepared for the next journey. I unlearned so much that, if I had brought it all with me to Paris, I would have been just as unhappy there as I was in Ontario.

Life is not meant to be easy, and struggles are not meant to stop you in your tracks and cause you to give up on the course. It is meant to be a lesson in personal strength and personal growth, and it helps us to develop the skills we need to learn in order to move through these challenges. The Claudia who was lamenting about re-

WHAT ACCEPTANCE LOOKS LIKE

signing her mortgage and not having Paris in her immediate grasp would not have been ready for Paris at the time. The learning that happened over those years, and the spiritual knowledge gained over that period of time, is what truly prepared me for what was to come.

The Universe knew that. God knew what timing was essential for maximum growth. Source knew what I needed, *internally,* to make the next chapter in my book of life the best that it could possibly be.

"Blessed is the person who has struggled. He has found life."

   - *The Gospel of Thomas*

CHAPTER THREE
WHAT RISK LOOKS LIKE

The stages of healing, recognition, and unlearning that I was experiencing were opening me up to a greater connection to Source and, with that, my spiritual gifts began to emerge with incomparable strength. As my connection began to grow, I started offering my services of Tarot reading to friends, family, and strangers on the internet for nothing, or for a small donation. I did this as an apprenticeship, if you will, but mostly so I could channel the healing that I was doing into helping others heal as well.

One of the most important things that I learned through my healing and through my new discernment of the spiritual sources, was that the true purpose of spiritual practice and spiritual gifts was not to feed the ego, rise above the others, and propel you to internet fame. Spiritual practice is meant to be in service to fellow man or woman, with the intention of making the world a better place by aligning with the God energy.

That being said, one crucial matter of importance that is central to this true path of spirituality, is to perform without recognition and without attachment to results. Kind acts, service to others, and the sharing of Love is meant to be done without external validation or expecting a certain outcome (that usually works in your favour). I stopped feeding my ego by bragging on social media about my successes, my service to man or my gifts, and I stopped performing acts of kindness expecting them to be returned or expecting praise as a result. When I began to focus on planetary betterment without needing to inflate my ego as a result of that work, my gifts truly amplified beyond measure.

This is how the Hindu concept of Dharma functions - Ascension is tied to selfless action. As you Ascend, naturally, your spiritual gifts begin to develop more strongly. One of the ways that I began to create a clear and direct connection to my guides and angels was through my dreams.

In January 2018, a week before my 30th birthday, I had a very vivid dream as I slept. In this dream, I was dragging luggage through the streets of Paris and using the GPS on my phone to find "my apartment." After dropping off my luggage with excitement, I ran back down the stairs and started to explore "my city". I bought bread from "my boulangerie" and was calling my friends to let them know that they could go on exploring without me, because I planned to stay (live) here for a while.

I woke up completely soaked in tears. Everything about this dream felt *real*, far more than any night reverie of Paris I had experienced in the past. I was *there*. I felt the cobblestone beneath my feet. I smelled the pastries in the shops. I heard the accordion player on the street. I nuzzled my way through tourists, all the while knowing I wasn't one of them. I was actually there and there was no denying it, hence my tears upon awakening in my bed in Hamilton, Ontario.

I had two options when I woke up that morning:

- Shake it off and continue on with my day because it was just a dream, or;
- Allow how realistic and authentic that dream felt to be my drive to *just go for it* and recognize it as the sign it was meant to be from my guides.

I chose the second option.

As I have mentioned, I had a steady and secure position as a Special Education Teacher within a public school board in Ontario. In fact, when I awoke from that Parisian dream, it was on a weekday and I had to get ready to go to work. I had to get ready to fall back into that routine after just having had the very real taste of Paris taken away from me. Again, thoughts of, "Is this really what I want to do until I turn 60?" rang through my head, even louder than they had before. The answer was no.

So, what was I going to do about it?

Mornings at my teaching job always started with a planning period that I typically used to mark student work or create lessons for the day. On this day, I used my planning time to search online: "English jobs in Paris." The first results lead me to a babysitting company. I could hear the voices of the critics already: "How embarrassing", "That's so below you", "What a downgrade", "Why would anyone give up such financial security in Canada for a babysitting job in France?"

Although at that moment, I didn't care. I saw it as an open door to my dream, a beginner's opportunity, and I grabbed it, applying on the spot. Within just a few hours, I got an email back asking if I was available for a job interview via video chat in two days. I said yes. I was already feeling the excitement of accepting this interview which was something I hadn't felt prior in my life, not even when I reached significant milestones and checked items off my life-list. This joy was new. This joy was already overwhelming.

Two days later, I got the job offer at the end of the interview. Moments after that, I sent an email to Human Resources and said: "I am leaving."

RISK TAKES SACRIFICE

In addition to my teaching job, I was "side hustling" by writing blogs and managing a small "bookstagram" account where I was being offered books and products to review. I was also discussing starting a social media marketing company with a friend and I was offering my Tarot readings to clients. I still had #girlboss on my Instagram profile bio and I was consistently on the hunt for opportunities to make a bit more money. I had bought into the idea that a self-made and happy woman is always working, is always on the move, and is always on the hunt.

If I was going to move forward with allowing my dream to be the push, the catalyst, to just go for it, I was going to have to go against all of that. Dropping everything based upon a (literal) dream is a risk that is difficult to calculate. Everything I had financially established for myself, career-wise, in Canada, would need to be abandoned. I would have to be ready to start from scratch, all over again.

Manifesting a life that ultimately brings you true, authentic, and soul-centered joy requires being okay with a lot of loss in the process. This could include the loss of friends, relationships, family support, jobs, possessions and, most importantly, financial stability. A true risk isn't a leap from comfortable to comfortable; it requires sacrifice and losses. If you are not okay with that, you are never going to be able to move in the direction of manifesting the very best life for yourself.

The Universe did allow me one small win when it came to this abandonment - my work allowed a one year unpaid sabbatical and, while I wouldn't be returning to the job I left, I wouldn't be removed from their system either. Still, I was giving up a very steady monthly income, I would no longer be contributing to my pension and I'd be sacrificing my healthcare to pursue something on the other side of the world.

In fact, the babysitting job I had just been offered would be paying me nine Euros an hour for only 20 hours a week. That's 180 Euros a week, not including the taxes that would be deducted. I was essentially going from what I made in a day of work to making that in a week. While I was offered the grace of the security of a sabbatical, this was nothing short of a great financial loss.

In general, in France, the minimum monthly wage sits at double what I would be making. If you have never

WHAT RISK LOOKS LIKE

looked into real estate in France, unless you are willing to be living in a 10 meter square cube with a shared washroom in the hallway of the building, you are never going to find anything for less than 700 Euros a month. Add the cost of food on top of that, the insurance I would be paying to cover my trip and, of course, the expenses of living out this experience, I would be living at a loss - a huge loss. I would be going into the red, every month. Even knowing this, I proceeded with my plan to listen to that dream.

North Americans, in particular, get very used to and comfortable with a certain kind of living. They fall into their lifestyle and, even though it doesn't bring them joy, they think it's what they *need*. They believe that stepping outside of their comfort zone would bring them more suffering in the long run. In laymen's terms, they are incapable of doing what those in finance call a risk assessment.

I considered the financial beating that I would be taking to be similar to a penny stock investment. While you can never anticipate if the penny stock will take off the way some financial advisors feel it might, I considered this to be worth every risk. So much so, that I bet my entire life on it. The danger with penny stock investments is that they can turn out to be completely useless over a few weeks, months, or years, and you can see all your money essentially flushed down the drain.

Dreams require that kind of risk as well.

If you feel a tugging at your heartstrings -whether it's to go someplace different, build a life in a new nation, open a small business, create for a living - if that tugging is persistent over the years, I am telling you, it's worth the investment. If you can look at the bigger picture, you'll realize that the only thing that is holding you back from moving forward with this dream is the "what if." In other words, what's holding you back is fear.

Fear is a human emotion that we can either listen to and allow to control the direction of our lives, or we can push it to the side and trust in God and ourselves. Fear is not something felt *on the other side;* it is a completely human experience and it is thrown in our direction to steer us away from the soul blueprint we agreed to before our incarnation on earth. When your life is headed in the direction of *exactly where you are meant to be,* you will notice your fear begin to amplify. This is no coincidence.

Lower energies that like to keep us trapped in the "just okay," ego, and the enticing world of comfortable, like having us stay in a zone where we fall into human routine and no longer pursue our dreams. That's because this space isn't really soul-satisfying and we look to materialism, to drugs and alcohol, to social media, and to toxic relationships to help fill the void. In my opinion, comfortable helps fund the darkness.

Dreams are soul memories, and soul memories help

WHAT RISK LOOKS LIKE

us heal karma, learn lessons, and Ascend. A soul memory is the blueprint of our life, the purpose and goal we agreed to before we were incarnated on earth. It is the path we *want* to transverse so our spirit can rise in this life and the next. Yet, for many people, it has been forgotten or pushed to the side by fear.

Ascension doesn't benefit these lower energies; keeping us trapped in human karmic cycles benefits them far more. It satiates them. And so, often our dreams come stacked with these risks - such as extreme financial loss - which trigger our fears and result in us keeping our feet planted and not moving forward. Darkness wins, we suffer in this life, and are doomed to repeat soul-history in the next.

Realigning with our soul blueprint is the only way to truly live out our life purpose and find complete fulfillment. However, if it were easy, everyone would be realigned and living their dreams right now! It takes a truly aware person to say, "Something about this life doesn't feel right and I'm going to do something about it."

This is the first step to realigning with the plan that our souls agreed to.

The next step is acceptance of the fact that this will not be easy. I always say that if the path is easy, doesn't take much sacrifice on your part, and doesn't bring about those fear-based thoughts, then it's not your true soul blueprint. It's not your real life purpose. Much like mental and emotional healing, this process takes hard work and can be painful, but that's essentially how progress works.

The etymology of progress breaks down to:

A. Going on, the action of walking forward;

B. Growth, development, advancement to higher stages.

Without fearlessly walking - which often involves moving through thorny, rough, and uneven terrains (our roadblocks, losses, and challenges) - we cannot advance to the higher stages of our being (Ascension through following our life purpose).

We cannot develop and grow in *comfortable*. Growth and development require challenges; a seed pushes through soil, a butterfly emerges by breaking through its cocoon. You do not build muscle by lying in bed, you build muscle by lifting weights that get heavier and heavier as time goes on. Following our dreams involves the same ladder-like assessment of challenges and disappointments.

When you connect with your Higher Self, it will speak to you in whispers and nudges that focus on a joyful dream with an overall air of betterment. When you respond to these whispers, you are acting on an energy of Love. Aligning to Source means that the actions we are taking to reach these dreams are all paths that lead to

WHAT RISK LOOKS LIKE

God. When you are driven by a dream, and do not allow fear to distract you from that dream, you become unattached to material losses or gains, failure, or disappointment - you just focus on the dream as your goal or intention. So long as you are taking action in the direction of that intention, you are aligning with Divine energy and will be rewarded for your efforts.

The key here is action; you are not rewarded with abundance without sufficient ego-less action and trust in the Universe. If you begin to manufacture expectations about how you want the Universe to play it all out for you because of your fears (of financial loss, of relationship loss, of security loss, etc.) then you are headed in the direction of disappointment, my friend.

With moving to Paris, even though I *knew* that I would be in the red on a monthly basis, something inside me told me to trust the sign, act on the opportunity, and do it anyway. I said to myself, *"It will work itself out"*, without any outline of how that was going to be. I aligned with the Source energy that was driving my dream and I leaped into it.

You will find that once you jump, and trust that the Universe has strapped a parachute to your back, you'll never regret it. I know I didn't.

THE TRANSFORMATIONAL PATH

THE HUSTLE IS A LIE

A big lesson that I needed to learn from the financial losses that I was planning to take on, was the fact that Hustle Culture is a lie. We are being consistently fed content that tells us to keep working, keep busy (to the point of breaking), and to keep looking for opportunities to *make money*. Money making is the focus of Hustle Culture; it does not discuss hustling for your mental health, hustling to build healthier relationships or hustling for joy. It associates The Hustle as being the way you - and others - could easily define whether you are living a successful life, or whether you are not. If you're not hustling, you're not successful - plain and simple.

A lot of hustling happens behind the scenes, so the key to this culture is to identify a few important placeholders:

- Consistently telling people you are "hustling"
- Posting photos or videos of you at your desk, in your home office, running errands for a side business or brainstorming your next business venture
- Mentioning hustling, working hard or being a #GirlBoss in your online profiles

- Complain about "giving up things" (like vacations) because you are so dedicated to your work
- Showing off what hustling has "got you" by posting materialistic things purchased with the "money you earned"; bonus points if these were big ticket items like a car or a condo

Basically, Hustle Culture is a performative experience. It's not something you do quietly, for yourself, it's something you do to gain recognition and approval from others.

A greater issue with Hustle Culture is that it is a lie meant to keep you trapped in a grinding routine until you burn out. The reason for this is that the more you hustle, the more exhausted you become, which in turn leads you to burnout, and that results in you purchasing *quick fixes*. Hustle Culture feeds consumerism!

Ever notice that the people who are *hooked by the hustle* are the same people posting weekend (or weekday) photos and videos of their overconsumption of alcohol? Ever notice how they are more likely to buy into the spiritual items and ideas that promise instant results, *manifestation,* the success they will have with the Law of Attraction, and other nonsense quick fixes? Those people who are in love with the hustle often fall into drug usage or materialism as a way to escape the burn out.

I was no different.

In fact, the most substantial piece of my performance that I used to show others to demonstrate how dedicated I was to the hustle was my house. I had a house before most people my age and I used that to demonstrate my commitment to being a #GirlBoss. So, when I had made the decision to move to Paris, I came to the realization that I would no longer have this placeholder of my success; being a homeowner would no longer be a central part of my identity that I could brag about to others. It became far easier to release this concept when it became clear to me how absolutely ridiculous it all was.

People really had a difficult time believing that I was willing to give up the comforts of being a homeowner for a cube-sized apartment in Paris where the rent was more than my mortgage. Even more so, people truly couldn't understand how I could go from making over 75 thousand dollars a year to making nine Euros an hour for 20 hour work weeks. They didn't know how the girl who bragged about the hustle, and her multitude of milestone successes, could abandon all of that and move across the world just to follow a dream.

To me, that was the revelation of what real hustling was; projecting yourself in the direction of your dreams and joys. The hustle should not make you feel burned out or as though you are always on the race track, running to reach the next checkpoint. The hustle should make you feel consistently joyful and fulfilled. And, when you are living from a frequency of joy, God recognizes that you trusted the process and the Universe rewards you for it. You are hustling for happiness, not for monetary wealth and material successes.

In fact, the etymology of the noun hustle is *to push activity in the interest of success*.

At this turning point in my life, knowing that success was clearly not what I had once defined it to be and that success is actually measured far better through joy and a lust for life, *hustle for happiness* made perfect sense to me. It also made me feel like a better person overall. One who brought far more value to her community and relationships. When I was joyful, it radiated out to others and motivated them to also find and chase their joy.

So, when I put up my house for sale, I designed a paper cheque from the Universe to me. On this cheque, I wrote that the Universe was rewarding me with wealth to spare and share. In a way, it was me asking God for a sign about whether traversing this path was exactly where Source wanted me to go, despite all the negativity I was receiving from others.

On the cheque, I also wrote $10,000.

My house had five offers within the first 24 hours and one was exactly $10,000 over asking.

Quite clearly, the Universe had responded - I had my sign.

LEARNING WHO TRULY SUPPORTS YOUR DREAMS

When joy began to flood my life, as the Universe started to present the steps of my journey to me, it came with the revelation as to who in my life I would want to keep by my side as I walked this path to my dreams. Unfortunately, often one of the downfalls of listening to the Universe and putting in the work to pursue your own happiness also reveals many judgmental individuals.

I was dating someone at the time when I decided I was going to listen to my (literal) dream and move forward with following my (soul) dream to Paris. Granted, this individual was already someone deep within the category of toxic; they had addict tendencies, they were an expert manipulator and gaslighter, and they were emotionally abusive while disguising themselves as the constant victim of life. Needless to say, this was already a partnership that I would soon learn to release and heal from, whether I stayed in Canada or not.

Anyone who had taken a moment to get to know me to the depths of my spirit, knew that writing in Paris was my life goal. Perhaps most people viewed it as a pipe dream that would never manifest but that was their prerogative. I, on the other hand, knew it was my purpose and everything within my life was driving me in that direction. This boyfriend was no different; from day one he was aware of this dream and he called it, "cool" and, "exciting."

When I finally woke up from that hyper-realistic dream and said, "This is what I'm doing," imagine my shock when he *shamed* me for it. If things were bad before, he turned up the amp to eleven.

He began to call me selfish and unreasonable. He ridiculed me and said that I was only going across the world to meet a new man and start a new life (truly an insult considering this dream was about a spirit longing that was solely mine, so this comment belittled me and it's purpose). And he asked me "how [I] could do that [to him]" as if this was about him, at all. He used me following my dreams as an excuse to treat me even worse, to justify his alcohol and drug use and blame it on me, and to gaslight me even further. He equated me following my dreams to intentionally trying to destroy him, even threatening to commit suicide if I left him.

It is important to mention here that we hadn't built anything substantial together; not that a substantial foundation should prevent you from pursuing dreams, anyway. We had a relationship that was off-and-on endlessly. He was unemployed, broke, and practically living rent-free in my home while playing video games most days. He ate the food that I bought because he had no cash and didn't qualify for credit. He benefited from me being trapped in Ontario far more than I benefited from anything within the partnership. I, a compassionate and empathetic person, had still not completely learned about the danger of leeches. However, I had let other depressive and lowly men trap me before and, this time, I generated enough strength to put myself and my joy completely first. Unapologetically.

Of course, when you are making a huge decision that involves dropping your life to begin a new one in a new country, negative comments - no matter how absurd or insulting they are - truly add to the fear. And he knew that; he did that consciously. Because this, unfortunately, is yet another challenge and lesson the Universe tests you on - to truly see how ready you are for the sacrifices you're about to make and the journey you're about to take.

If there isn't any fear, you're not headed in the right direction. So, I used his commentary and cruelty to fuel my great move, turning the fear into excitement; it helped me to end things with him, once and for all.

He wasn't the only person to remove their mask and show me their true colours when I made the decision to move to France. I had girlfriends in my life who reacted to the news of this move in some disappointing ways, including:

- Ridiculing that I was going to, "start with a few months to feel (it) out," telling me it wasn't a real move at all
- Pretending it wasn't happening and never asking me about it or talking to me about it (despite it being the most exciting moment of my entire life)
- Talking to others behind my back about my great move to, "follow [my] dreams" while whispering that it wouldn't last

True friends celebrate your successes and your strength to follow your dreams. Relationships are not formed to be selfishly beneficial; they are to help the other person's spirit advance, selflessly. The reason you create friendships, bonds, and partnerships is for growth and betterment. So, when you see the soul you are bonded with advancing, even if it's ahead of you, your duty as a friend is to encourage them and honor them.

The purpose of true friendship in community, is to help you traverse through your challenges and difficulties and to have a team that pushes you forward when you're on the precipice of growth. Being reincarnated as humans, means that we require this community to help us learn lessons and advance as a species. When some girlfriends in my life were exposing their jealousy and disappointment in my personal advancement and belittling my courage to risk so much to pursue this soul-calling, it was heartbreaking.

I did not need them to project their resentment at their own inability to put their dreams first. I did not need them to project their judgment on the decisions I was making for myself. I needed them to be a pillar and a presence of positivity, considering they were all massively aware of the role that Paris played in my life, in my trauma healing, and knowing how long I had been carrying this dream.

That being said, while many masks and negative faces were revealed, the faces of loving and true friends also came forward. My foundation of support became stronger with the knowledge I gained that allowed me to sift through which relationships were positive and aligned to mutual betterment and which I could let go of. It was now a perfect opportunity to say goodbye to any relationship that was taking more from me than it was giving.

MASTERING FORGIVENESS

For me, falling away from many of my relationships and partnerships highlighted the human need for us to be loved and, in the process, have our hopes and dreams supported by those we surround ourselves with. It also highlighted that the baggage of resentment, frustration, or toxic opinion was not something I wanted to travel with to Paris. This *"ah-ha!"* moment became a spiritual lesson because I realized just how important it was to forgive these people, lest I carry that energetic weight with me.

Though the process of true forgiveness was one I began to master when going through my court case with my sexual assailant, it was strengthened as I released many people from my life prior to departing from Canada.

You cannot blame people who are frustrated with feeling stuck in their own lives and who project this resentment onto you for *unsticking yourself*. They aren't there yet. They haven't reached that moment of trusting themselves enough to move forward with their own dreams and to jump confidently towards the signs handed to them from the Universe. Their anger is not actually towards you, at all. Their anger is with themselves.

In fact, we cannot blame people, in general, for where they are in their stages of healing. Feelings such as anger, jealousy, resentment, animosity, or spite are not normal states of being. They are often external projections of internal frustration or unhealed trauma.

Responding with anger towards these individuals will never lead to a neutral energetic understanding of one another. Your only option is to respond with love.

Love, as I have already stressed, is the most powerful energetic vibration that you can work on because it is truly the vibration of Source. Love and it's counterpart, Forgiveness, do not tell people that their actions are okay, or that you accept them, but rather they tell people that you understand they have work to do and you wish them well on that journey.

Responding with love means you energetically release the ties you have to this person and do not allow what they are trying to propel in your direction to disturb your peace. You cut the etheric energetic cords through love and forgiveness. You no longer owe these people anything and they no longer have an influence on your serenity.

Over the years, I have learned that we are all at different stages of our healing journey. It is not my responsibility to judge how people react, emotionally, to frustrations with their external world. This includes how people react to me. I cannot make people like me, understand me, or not have anger, resentment, or jealousy towards me. The best I can do is recognize that *this isn't about me at all* and this is their own projection of their insecurities and unhealed issues.

If you allow people to disturb your serenity with their

insecurities, you're doing a disservice to your Spirit and you're allowing them power and control where they otherwise have none. In the end, we don't really have to understand one another. We just need to let others live their most peaceful and joyful life as they work towards their healing. Wish them the best of luck and release; this is best done through forgiveness and the power of the energy of Love.

People act in this way towards you out of fear, and fear is a disease that causes dis-ease. As the Buddhists believe, people act this way out of an attachment to suffering and dissatisfaction. It is much harder to break the cycle of misery than it is to just allow it to continuously repeat, and others will resent you when you have the strength to do it. They are far too fearful to break this cycle. The only way to combat fear is with love.

To leap with this much faith and have no expectations for how it may look, and to let go of everything that once kept you comfortable, is very similar to the path to nirvana or enlightenment. It shows great wisdom to *"let go and let God"*, and this will not sit well with everyone you know. Do not let them project their own fears onto your journey in an attempt to hold you back from this path of self-discovery and dream manifestation. Just respond with love and compassion, and release.

"…When you know that language, it's easy to understand that someone in the world awaits you, whether it's in the middle of the desert or in some great city. And when two such people encounter each other, and their eyes meet, the past and future become unimportant. There is only that moment, and the incredible certainty that everything under the sun has been written by one hand only. It is the hand that evokes love, and creates a twin soul for every person in the world. Without such love, one's dreams would have no meaning."

- *The Alchemist by Paulo Coelho*

CHAPTER FOUR
FAIRY TALES ARE REAL

Healing, releasing, and growing in compassion allows for a strengthening of your spiritual connection. My energetic connection to Source was multiplying at a rate I had difficulty keeping up with, but it truly helped me understand that I was supported along this journey. After eight years of wishing, hoping, and praying for this to come to light, I wasn't going to let anything stop me. It was time to hop on that plane and make a life for myself in Paris.

In August 2018, I did just that. I cried tears of joy - and fear - as I left my parents in the airport. Not for a vacation, but to start a journey for myself, on my own, in Paris.

Although when I arrived, everything seemed to go pretty wrong.

I don't believe in coincidences, and you know by now that I truly believe challenges and frustrations are just another attempt by the Universe to "bulk you up" - spiritually, of course. I will liken it, again, to muscle building; even when everything seems to be going right, your faith will be tested in a momentary crash. There is an important lesson under this disappointment that will help you unravel karmic or present-day lessons. The Universe *wants* you to "punch" through this. Like how I wrote in my journal after arriving in Paris, "It's okay. Just laugh or else you'll cry. Don't forget about gratitude for the Universe for helping this happen. No one promised it would be easy."

Within 24 hours of arriving into France, I was faced with numerous frustrations: my landlord decided he was "too tired from vacation" for the early check-in and he made me wait outside my apartment with three suitcases for two hours; the French bank account I was intending to open in order to effectively receive my salary called me to let me know it "couldn't be done" and it "wasn't [their] problem"; my apartment was smaller in-person than online - and the washroom filtered into the kitchen (gross); one of my two credit cards from Canada wasn't being recognized by French pay systems; one of the families I was assigned to work, after searching my history online and viewing the rainbow flags in my profile and the tattoos on my skin, refused to work with me and I was under an emergency reassignment for a new family.

Needless to say, the thoughts going through my head as all this stress mounted just hours after my arrival had me wondering, "Did I do the right thing? Was this the biggest mistake of my life? What happens now? I am truly alone and overwhelmed."

What I've come to discover is that God will present to you all that you hope to manifest in a way that feels imperfect for a few reasons:

- To teach you to be more specific with how you want life to unfold
- To show you that sometimes dreaming about that "next best thing" isn't really as dreamy as you've made it out to be in your head
- To help you develop resilience and learn more lessons that help you advance towards your ultimate betterment
- To teach you new skills that force you to *work for what you want*

So, I took a deep breath and I embraced the nerves, fear, and the frustrations and said to myself, "This is what I wanted, and this is a part of living in France"

Eventually I'd continue to learn, more and more, how true that statement really was.

When I woke up the next morning, with far less stress and anxiety, and took a walk through my beautiful Marais neighbourhood, I wrote this in my journal:

> "Wow. This is the city I live in. This is the city I am currently calling home. It is beyond spectacular and beyond inspiring. I'm glad to be alive and living this, and breathing this, and doing my dream-thing like I always said I would."

I felt a sense of accomplishment and pride that nothing prior had ever seemed to fill me with. This was entirely my own dream, my own goal, my own milestone... but it was also so much more than that. For the first time in my life, I felt at home and I could physically, emotionally, and spiritually feel that I was planting roots that were being nourished by the Universe. I knew that this was where I would grow.

This city would be the place where I would bloom so intensely that I'd touch the sky and find the Kingdom of God within me. It Awakened within me a Divine connection that I could not anticipate. I wrote this in my journal:

"Something wakes within me as the sun rises, hitting the beautiful blue rooftops that I see from the window of my apartment. Something I can feel deep within my core. Something that escapes through my fingertips and flows down to my legs and calls me to move forward and onwards and towards what most invigorates me, what most sets my soul on fire.

Sitting at the Seine's edge, I was moved to tears. I am so happy. I don't remember the last time I was so overwhelmed with complete grace and appreciation for life. Each day I feel it more and more. Each day I admire this life that I am living by stepping outside of myself, observing, feeling gracious, and then heading back in deep so I don't miss a second.

I am so unequivocally grateful for the life I'm living right this moment. Everything I've ever done, every lesson I've learned from mistakes I've made, every struggle, every success, has led to me being here… right here. Who I am in this moment is all that matters. Who I've been is just a memory. Right now, as I write this, my heart swells with gratitude and life is beautiful and I am swimming in happiness.

I forgive anyone who has ever wronged me. How happy I am right now is the greatest revenge I could ever give them. And it comes from a place of compassion. So the whole Universe wins.

If I take anything back with me from Paris, let it be this: may I carry with me the spirit of this city that endlessly inspires and moves me, so that lust for life exists no matter where I call "home."

I am so completely and utterly in love with this city and how it's made me feel. Paris, you are truly mine, but my darling, I am yours, all yours. I will always be yours. May my steps along your streets move you in such a way as you have done for me. These days will never be forgotten. You will be the song I sing till the day I die. I am endlessly grateful that I got to love you like this, in this new way. You've written your name on my soul and I belong to you."

Absolutely everyone deserves to feel how I felt when writing that passage. Following your dreams, harnessing

Love, healing your wounds, and practicing forgiveness is the way to manifest those feelings for yourself.

MONEY ISN'T EVERYTHING

Thankfully, a new family quickly jumped at hiring me as their English babysitter and my work was back to a steady 20 hours per week. The children I worked with were so lovely and their personalities so diverse. The parents were just as excited to have a Canadian Special Education teacher working with their children. It was definitely a different work experience than sitting in an hour of traffic, pulling into a large drive-thru line up to get my morning fix, going into a school every day and then being bullied by colleagues, and berated by pretentious parents.

Instead, I was riding the metro and train like a local, grabbing snacks from the boulangerie on the way to the job, doing some shopping on Champs Elysees if I was running early, and playing with kids in beautiful Haussmannian buildings. There was an aura about my workspaces and work days that was completely different and, to top it off, I didn't have to take home marking or planning on the weekends.

In addition, the shorter hours meant I was able to dedicate more of my weekdays to writing, which was one of the primary catalysts for wanting to call myself a

Parisienne. All the writers that I admired had their stint in Paris and I wanted to join their literary ranks. My short work days allowed me to visit beautiful bookstores, gave me time to sit in cafes and journal and opened many hours up to exploration and adventure in the city of my dreams.

While I knew that living in the red was not sustainable long-term, I trusted that this was temporary and I was never closed off from more employment opportunities. I attended interviews and browsed job posting sites. I even made an effort to start a little side gig as an English language instructor. Although I wasn't hustling, not this time. Instead, I was *falling into grace.*

I reminded myself that I was living in the city of my dreams as I always hoped I would be, writing daily, and feeling immense amounts of gratitude for the foundation this was building for me.

You see, writing is my life purpose. I knew this from when I was just a kid. I was constantly creating magazines, writing poetry, designing picture books, and even creating novels as a young girl. There was always a whisper in my mind that said I could be a writer as an adult, but eventually that whisper was dulled away by the noise of, "writers don't make money," and, "an author is not a real career." So I pushed it aside and called it a hobby.

When you have correctly identified your life purpose

and started to live it fearlessly, the Universe rewards you. What you are saying by abandoning the comfortable life you were previously living and stepping into your soul calling is, "I trust you, Universe; you have assigned this task to me, and I will follow through with my path truly blind."

Trust and faith in the Universe is an energetic alignment to Source energy, and God floods abundance onto those who are able to tap into that and let it be their nourishment.

So, while I wasn't making a lot monetarily (at that moment), the abundance I had in all other aspects of my life was immeasurable and like nothing I had ever experienced before.

Back in Canada, I defined abundance and had abundance defined for me by others as being focused on financials. Wealth meant money, and that was the be-all and the end-all. Hustle Culture perpetuated this mentality, stressing the need for women to get their stacks and buy their high-end items. Now, as I've said before, money isn't bad. However, like all of life, any focus that is directed towards only one source is going to tip out of balance and going to cause chaos. An over-obsession with getting and holding onto money creates an energy of fear around loss, which blocks money from being pulled to you.

The happier you are, the less you focus on monetary

wealth, if at all. In fact, you gain a kind of understanding that, like everything else in life, this will ebb and flow as it desires without much input from you. The general energy of joy is one that is in alignment with Source and so, when you're happy and everything else in life seems to be going splendidly, it's no coincidence! You are creating an aura of abundance around your being and that helps other elements of goodness in life flow towards you. Eventually, that includes money!

While I wasn't really pocketing any excess money, I was content beyond measure and that distracted me from any concerns surrounding finances at all. I had the mentality that, for life to feel so good, the Universe wouldn't punish me with struggling beyond what I was capable of handling.

Life was harder because of my monetary loss living overseas, but my God has never been a cruel God. My God rewards people who trust that the Universe has their back and they're fully supported as they chase their joy and live out their life purpose. I knew this when I started my Parisian journey. I'm not sure how I knew this, but I knew it within the very core of my being.

When I was making steady and significant money in Canada, I was still completely unsatisfied with my life. The comfort of that wealth could not balance the disappointment in all other aspects of my being; my relationships were unfulfilled, my work was draining me,

I was eating poorly, I was spending money on stupid and unnecessary things, I was mentally in a dark space, and I was consistently searching for the "why" in everything I was doing. I used to wonder what the purpose of that routine and work-sleep-eat-work cycle was, because it seemed too mundane and depressing to have any answer at all.

Yet, here I was in Paris, walking the cobblestone streets of my dreams, eating food that was healthier and truly nourishing, achieving a work-life balance that I desperately needed, and finding the "why" in every inspirational corner. Even though I was in the red, I was so unbelievably joyful. I was joyful beyond measure.

True, unfiltered joy does expands out of you and infects and draws all others to live on the same energetic wavelength - the wavelength of the Divine, of Source, of God. Being able to share that energy and inspiration with others is more uplifting, long-lasting, and impactful than sharing any monetary wealth.

LEARNING WHAT LIFE WAS ABOUT - SOLO

Living in the city of my dreams awakened in me an attunement to the Divine energy of God which brought with it numerous lessons and insight that I couldn't have anticipated. The Buddhists truly believe that when you are living a life of compassionate joy that is selflessly shared with anyone you encounter, even through small gestures of kindness, you are rewarded with growing wisdom. I felt this in the very spirit of my being and I felt as though the Universe was rewarding me for bravely following my heart's desire.

Every building I passed, every garden I walked through, every new interaction with a stranger, every adventure I jumped into on my own, I felt as though I was gaining knowledge about the world that I didn't have previously. More importantly, I felt I was learning so much about myself. One of the most beautiful things I learned about myself was that I was fully and completely in love with my existence and didn't need a partnership to feel fulfilled or successful. I dropped that milestone from my checklist fearlessly, and I felt so free.

This freedom also brought me an ability to trust myself beyond measure. That meant I was unafraid of risk, unafraid of acting on a whim, unafraid of getting lost, unafraid of failure, and unafraid of listening to my intuition when it called to me. Since I learned to love myself so deeply by following my joy, I also learned not to take signs for granted.

One of these signs led me to Rocamadour.

Rocamadour is a small medieval town in France built into a cliff side. Most French people have never visited it and many wondered how I knew about it at all. The fact of the matter was that I didn't know about it, not really.

I was sending a voice-to-text SMS to someone and, after speaking for a minute or so, I looked down at my phone to correct any errors and send the message. There was only one word on my screen: *Rocamadour.* I sent this to the person I was texting, followed by, "What the hell is a Rocamadour?"

I quickly search for it online, only to discover it is a miracle-working site of the Black Madonna in France.

There are no coincidences. The Universe was speaking loud and clear. I was to trust myself and go there. It awoke even more passionate admiration for my own strength to follow where God was guiding me.

I wrote this in my journal in October 2018:

"Maybe I have been here before – walked these ancient streets. I wonder about this cobblestone beneath my feet. Has it been felt before? Could I have lived here? Could I live here, now? Could this small and sacred town be the home of my endless inspiration and my growth as a writer?

A wasp bumps into my carafe d'eau and I feel the same confusion – searching in a reflection of reality, to faraway places for what feels most right, most like home. Waiting for a miracle that reveals my soul purpose.

I don't know that it's Ontario. I don't know

that it's teaching. I don't know, I don't know, I don't know... but I don't feel that it is...

Has my gut ever led me astray before? No. It has been my greatest guide. Wiser than my mind, than my heart. Both having me be a slave to emotion... and yet, is inspiration not driven by emotion?

I am so confused.

People come to the Black Madonna seeking answers and miracles. I come to her with the same:

Why?

Where?

How?

When?

With whom?

With whom – I'm open, truly open, to just me. I am becoming immensely comfortable on my own. I love myself. I love the peace I bring myself. I will not settle for anyone who tries to shake up my relationship with myself. I am happy alone. Intimacy with just anyone – revealing all precious sides of myself to another – does scare me. But that is a topic for another day...

For now, I sit here at this table outside Le

Bistrot Bar in Rocamadour. I look out and I see what I believe life is about...
SIMPLICITY AND LOVE."

This revelation was immense. It was truth that had been spoken about by sages and wise men numerous times before, but this time it came to be shared with me. Life is not a complex problem meant to be fixed; the solution to all of the chaos, confusion, pain, suffering, and trauma lies in alignment with the Love energy of God. It is so simple!

Rocamadour did end up showing me my soul purpose and the Black Madonna was miracle-working; my clairaudient gifts were turned on while I was there and I am forever grateful that I trusted the sign, and trusted myself, enough to go on that adventure.

(I speak more about this clairaudient connection later on in this book.)

It was revealed to me that my soul purpose is to write; to write in a way that inspires others to make changes in their lives; to write about truth and to write about Light; to write so that others may be inspired to follow their dreams, that direction always being towards the light. I must be a guide, a beacon of Truth, a coach of Light and Love.

Having tuned into that and accepted it, I wrote the

following passage in my journal upon my return to my Parisian apartment:

"There is an overwhelming wave of utter disbelief and surrealism when a dream, years in the making, manifests itself into completion. And you are walking streets no longer as a tourist, but as one who is another blood cell swimming through the veins of the city.

When all your idols spoke of this life and your eyes would water at the thought of making that your reality as well, and then, in what feels like a blink of an eye, you are living that life…

And then the moments of self-doubt and isolation follow, because when God speaks, the devil wants you to doubt His beauty and triumph.

But I'll overcome that as well. And I am endlessly grateful.

People credit hard work to this happening, but I credit God, the Universe, everything greater than myself, including my own willpower.

The Universe presented me with the opportunity and I listened and leaped before I had a chance to test the waters.

Thank the heavens that I did.

I am swimming in bliss.

I just want to be authentically me, truly me, made of stardust, and sparkling for all to see. I want to step outside the box, I want to do what makes me happiest, I want to live comfortably but love each moment, not waste each moment, enjoy each moment, worship every moment. I want to find a way to make writing my living. I want to manifest it. I want others to read my work and say, "This has changed my life."

I want to change lives in a positive way. I want to help others see their own Light, so that they can move others as well.

As a teacher, I was told I changed lives. But now I want to inflict change in a new way. I want to reach new people."

The simplicity of this soul purpose is that I no longer need to worry about checklists, milestones, or hitting goals along a set timeline; all I need to do is to tune-in, write honestly and authentically (simply), and trust that these words will reach those who need to hear them.

I would later discover that these written words became central to my spiritual business.

That is confidence in the Divine and confidence in myself. That is Love. And, if you're reading this right now, that is faith manifested.

The Universe told me my words would change lives, and now I just needed to trust the Divine's timing as I learned well enough to do. I had a life purpose to align with and it was mine, alone, to follow and live out.

Knowing this, I was actually ready to return to Canada, so I planned my return for December when I would be able to make a more finalized decision about where I intended to live out my future, now that I had this profound information. That meant only two more months in Paris, and I was okay with that.

Although, of course, just as you've come to accept things as they are, God always has another plan...

MY HEART WAS IN PARIS

Remember the family who discriminated against me and decided not to work with me? And remember the new family that was eager to have me watch their children? What I initially saw as a frustration, roadblock, and insult to my ego ended up being a Divine plan I would have never anticipated.

Always trust the plan.

I stepped quite fully into the acceptance of a life lived alone, having come to the realization of the true purpose of relationships through this journal entry:

"If I eventually choose to grow old with someone, I want to be with someone who inspires me in the same way that Paris (and the surrounding area) does. I'm not asking for endless conversation or a pseudo-intellectual with the need to prove themselves through pointless banter and self-praise. But the mere presence of them, the energy they exude into the universe, is one that inspires others to know them. It's an energy that encourages others to be a reflection of compassion and passion. I don't think I could settle for anything less.

I want to look into eyes that give me the same rush of the heart that I get standing at the top step of the Chateau de Versailles, as I look out to the endless garden. I want to feel their breath along my neck, and feel the same as I do when Paris winds caress me there; complete freedom, and yet a sense of security and a feeling of home. I want their touch to feel as safe and as invigorating as each step in the Jardins du Luxembourg makes me feel.

But I also want to do the same for them. When they are with me, I want them to feel a greater sense of purpose in the universe. And I want my energy to endlessly fuel them, lift them, elevate their spirit.

For if we are not constantly bettering one another, what is the point?"

So, of course, one fine Thursday evening in November, my new Parisian family declared that they wanted to set me up with their friend, Jordan.

My pride immediately said, "No, thank you," and I explained how this journey to Paris was mine to be traversed alone, how happy I was by myself, and how satisfied I was with a life that had no dramatics of partnerships (since that was all I was used to). However, when my client pulled out her phone and showed me a photo of the most handsome man with the most intense - and familiar - eyes, I quickly caved and agreed to pass along my phone number to him. I am a sucker for beauty!

My first communication with Jordan via text was making it clear that:

- I wasn't interested in a relationship
- I liked being single and adventuring on my own

- I was a peaceful and Zen person who wished to avoid bringing stress and dramatics into my life, as relationships often can
- But let's grab a glass of wine to make his friends, and my clients, happy.

Jordan agreed with me. In fact, he was pretty much on the same page with a lot of the sentiments I was sharing with him. Our text messages were very honest, direct, and transparent right from the start. There was minimal flirting and we continued our conversation until early in the morning hours with a friendly and approachable tone. We agreed to meet at a tapas bar called Workshop, just down the street from me, that weekend - November 10th 2018.

As I walked up to the building and saw him standing outside, waiting for me, my eyes met his and, I swear to you, I heard a whisper that said, "This is it."

Within twenty minutes of sitting and talking with one another, I knew from the very depths of my spirit that this was my soulmate. There was not a doubt in my mind; every cell within me was screaming it. In twenty minutes, I felt like I knew him for 20 thousand years. The transparency and authenticity with which he poured out his spirit flooded me and I didn't drown, I swam in it. I swam in his warm waters with a contentment I cannot describe.

We spoke for three hours over one bottle of wine. I spilled an entire glass of red on myself and didn't care at all, I just wanted to dive back into his seas. (He later told me that the confidence with which I shrugged off an otherwise embarrassing moment was incredible; I recall saying to him, "Oh well, I hope you like the smell of wine!")

Near the end of our conversation, he began to reach out and caress my hand with his. His hands felt like home. I knew those hands. I swear to you, I did.

When we left Workshop, he turned me around and kissed me with a familiar softness and grace that made my whole heart sing. I stared deep into his eyes and saw my entire future reflected back at me. We laughed and embraced one another and I heard the laughter of the father of my children - something I never dreamt of or wanted prior to him. I held him and I felt the stillness of the world and the simplicity of Divine Love. He was everything and all things and, for the first time, I felt safe in the arms of a lover because it all felt *so easy.*

I remember texting my friends the next morning that I found "The One" and one of Jordan's friends later told me that he had done the same with them.

Our first night together, I looked him in the eyes and, without fear or hesitation, I told him, "I think you are my soulmate." We spent each day together after that. On the second day, he gave me the keys to his apartment and

FAIRY TALES ARE REAL

told me to call it home. On the third day, I told him I loved him and he held me and said the same - three words he had never said to another human being before me.

Except, I was planning to return to Canada - I had booked the tickets - and he was planning on finding work in South Africa. And so I wrote this in my journal:

"I've changed my mind. I don't want to go back to Canada. I've found my home in Paris. I've found my home in a set of brown eyes as deep as the Pacific ocean. I've found my home in skin that, when pressed up against my own, floods me with warmth and comfort. I've found my home in a soothing, sexy voice that never fails to get me thinking and exploring my own ideas, that has me blushing with endless compliments and words of affection. I've found my home when I run my fingers through his hair. I've found my home when I kiss his face and feel overwhelmed with emotion; emotions that scream, "this is it" and "better half" and "don't let go."

I've found my home in his vulnerability, in his beautiful laugh that makes his eyes squint and his bright smile show. I've found my home in words like, "mignon" and "mon petite bebe." I've found my home in a man named Jordan Alzraa, and my soul knew it from the moment I met him. It was the eyes. My eyes knew his eyes, like the patterns in our irises found their alignment and passion ignited immediately. Like every angel in my life screamed, "THIS IS WHO WE HAVE BEEN GUIDING YOU TO!" as soon as our cheeks touched in greeting.

Believe me, I am aware that this sounds insane. I am aware that people could read this or hear this and roll their eyes at the speed at which I am declaring my admiration for this person, but I have never spoken with greater certainty or clarity.

I know in my heart that this man is my soulmate; the person who, as the Greek philosophers said, was separated from me in creation, tossed across the ocean, and waiting for me to find him. And, ask anyone who knows me - they will tell you I didn't come here searching for anyone except myself. Yet, somehow, the Universe has aligned and we have arrived in one another's lives, and it's game over. It's done. I have met my (beautiful) doom. And I accept my fate. Because if my fate allows me additional moments with this man, than I will take all I can get.

I have known him for five days and feel as though I've known him for a lifetime. I have discovered more about this man in five days than past partners have revealed to me in years. And there are no rose-coloured glasses, I swear it. Everything from his past has brought him to me, here, in this moment, as he is. And for that, I am eternally grateful.

This man, in this moment with me, is better than anything I could have ever hoped for in a partner. He is beautiful, inside and out. His eyes are expressive and warm and loving and safe. I feel protected when wrapped up in his arms. It feels natural falling asleep next to him. I love the way he smells. I love the way he tastes. I love that our mindsets about life and living line up, but we have different interests to share with one another. I love listening to him speak. I love when he speaks English with his gorgeous accent. I adore when he speaks French; he looks more confident and comfortable when speaking his native tongue. It brings a smile to my face. I also love his smile; it radiates.

And I love how thoughtful and honest he is. I love his authenticity. I love that he is real with me and I love that he knows he can be real with me. I love when his fingers interlock with mine, when his lips collide with mine, when his body fits into mine like a puzzle piece. I love our sexual chemistry and comfort level. I love that our intimacy is sprinkled with moments of intense discussion, confession, and giggling. I love that in such a short period of time, this man already inspires me to be the best, most authentic version of myself, and to continue driving myself towards a life well-lived.

I love who I am when I am with him, and I love who I am when I am not; still independent, still free, still living my life as I need to live it. But now, like a river flows through a city, this new sense of drive flows through me, I am continuously moved by a sense of divine purpose, comfort, and joy when I think of him, of us.

I have read that you know it's your soulmate when everything falls into place instantaneously, but you are also met with challenges by the Universe, as though life is testing to see who will cave first and give up an opportunity at being with the person you're meant to be with. And we will have our own: I am going back to Canada, he is going to South Africa. But this is just a blip in the big picture. I am frustrated but unconcerned.

Because now I have felt what it means to find "The One" and I'm not willing to just toss it away or move onwards without him in my life. I simply can't. I have tasted him and now I wish to be drunk on him for eternity. I can no longer imagine a life without him in it, a bed without him next to me, a hand intertwined with any other fingers, my lips against the lips of any other... I simply can't.

Ask anyone who I was before all this and they will tell you that when I started dating someone, I still kept my options open, I kept my distance, I stayed cold. But no; I was exclusively his as soon as our eyes met over conversation. I am blinded by the sun that is he. No option exists but him. This is bliss, this is truth, this is real.

I need nothing else in this life as much as I need him beside me; journeying together, adventuring together, growing together, seeing success together, holding each other through failures, keeping one another endlessly warm. In every fantasy I have of my future, there he is now sprinkled. He exists, and to know he exists and I have had him as a part of my life, means I cannot experience my own existence in any other manner. It just won't do.

He is a nebula bursting within me. An

explosion of purpose that I never expected or imagined. He is someone I couldn't have even invented in my own mind. He is the living example of who I want to grow old with. Our connection is indescribable and unlike anything I've ever experienced.

    He is home. He is home. My home is when I am with him, and no other place will do, for he is home.

    I always said I was excited about finding where to truly set roots down in my life, because I am a lone wolf and a wanderer and an explorer and an endlessly curious dreamer. But now I know that the only roots I wish to bury deep are those that will be watered by his presence.

    Don't ask me how I know this after five days, but the Universe has spoken. It has whispered to my heart and I'm one to listen when it speaks. I said my heart was in Paris but I did not realize it would be a man. A man named Jordan Alzraa."

HEALTHY BONDS BRING ABUNDANCE

Within the first week, I was meeting Jordan's friends. They all told me that they have never been introduced to one of his partners before, and they've also never seen him *so changed*. And while it's true that I didn't know him before that fateful night, I immediately sensed a shift of energy.

You see, on our first date, after getting deep into our conversation together he said to me, "Listen, I have bad luck. It's almost like a curse, if you will. Nothing seems to go right for me, and there are always roadblocks in the way. But I'm a fighter, that you can be sure of."

I remember replying to him that my team of Angels and my constant good luck would balance everything out for him - I was happy to share it with him, too.

Jordan didn't come to me broken like my partners before him, but he came to me with a vulnerability and openness for wanting to be better. He knew how to identify what he didn't like in his life and he knew how he wanted to change it. This was no different to what I was also seeking through a healthy, spiritual relationship. I realized that it aligned with exactly what I wrote down a month prior: a true, Divine relationship should be founded upon betterment and growth, should avoid dramatics and should accept people as they are and not who they have the potential to become.

Even though Jordan told me he wasn't at his best, I loved him where he was and didn't expect more from him. Even in his perfectly imperfect state, our ideals, our goals, and our determination to grow and be better with a partner aligned perfectly. And that was enough.

Better than all that, everything with Jordan was truly easy. There was a sense of trust right off the bat that eliminated all jealousy and insecurities. There was a transparency that existed from the first date where we could be honest with each other and know there would be absolutely no judgment. Neither of us continued the bad habits that we would have otherwise kept in past relationships; for example, Jordan deleted his dating applications and I informed anyone I had a flirtatious relationship with that it would no longer be appropriate to continue our conversations.

Jordan knew that I would never judge him for anything in his past because it shaped him into the man he was with me, now, and I felt the same acceptance. We could laugh with one another and cry with one another without fear. We could do nothing together and experience endless joy and beautiful conversation. I didn't require continuous validation because I immediately felt safe and respected by him. We both fell quickly into the mindset of being aware of our significant other when making decisions in our life. We didn't go looking for reasons to argue, or things to criticize and bicker about.

We fell into this Divine level of comfort so quickly that not a single doubt existed in either of our minds about how, where, or when we would be able to build a life together. Considering all the change that was on the horizon, we just trusted the Universe. So much so that after two weeks of dating, Jordan suggested we get matching tattoos (his first!) of our Sun Sign constellation - Aquarius (we did it).

That kind of trust in God really does cause an energetic shift in the Universe. I already knew this through my journey, but Jordan quickly began to see the "luck in his life" start to change. He had no doubt about us and about the future we would have with one another, and this was a bond of trust that he never previously had with the Universe before he met me.

He was beginning to walk his path without needing to remove his blindfold. He took steps and leaps with a set belief that it would work out, because why else would two souls find one another and unite with such an explosion of firework-like energy and incredible certainty and strength? The Universe rewarded him for his faith.

I had an equivalent sense of trust in God and our bond. While such a commitment would have bored me in the past and had me push people away out of fear of not hitting that milestone fast enough, this time it was different. I wrote this in my journal:

> "To know *"The One"* means to never settle for life without them.

THE TRANSFORMATIONAL PATH

To have tasted heaven and then to give up on it would be the most foolish thing. What would life be if it were not nourished by his kisses, his hands on my body, his whispers in my ear? It would be like a tongue without the ability to taste. The world would have no life, no flavour. I would float through, as I once did, feeling as though all is bland, mediocre, uninspiring. Do not ask me to give up this dish which feeds my soul. I refuse.

He believes he is not deserving of happiness, calls himself cursed, but I have not found anyone who deserves it more. No one carrying the soul he has - one that cares endlessly about family, about friends, who so clearly puts them before himself without a second thought - deserves to be anything other than utterly content. The ones who continuously make sacrifices and put in effort for others often do not make time to seek out their own happiness - authentic happiness; not fleeting and temporary tastes, not purely corporal satisfaction, but lifetime happiness, eternal satisfaction, and contentment. He deserves to know that! I have found it for myself, he deserves the same.

It is my hope that I can be the catalyst to a life filled with these things. I hope I can help him realize he should no longer settle for a life without them. I hope we can adventure down a path of love and contentment and never stray. I want to be by his side through it all. I want to lift him out of his own darkness, take him into Light, and stay there with him.

If I could pull every star from the sky to add more light into his life, I would. But in the meantime, I will be the beacon he needs. I will love him with every fiber of my being in a way that pushes him to live his best and brightest life. I will be his support system. I will be his cheerleader. I will be his best friend and his partner in crime. I will be the one who pushes him and I will be the one who pulls him out of his own cynical mind. I will be his assistant and his teammate. I will be his lover and his comfort. I will be his safe space.

I will be all that he needs me to be and more than he never expected to need, because I know he would just as quickly take on these roles for me. I can feel that he wants to be the best version of himself for me and I can feel that he wants to love me the way I need to be loved.

I am so grateful.

His eyes show me how much he truly cares. I am so grateful.

THE TRANSFORMATIONAL PATH

I don't anticipate that the distance will be easy but we are not the first to do this and we won't be the last. What will drive me is the anticipation of making "forever" together, the deep trust I have in him, and the realization that we are meant to be. If I wasn't sure, I would be concerned about the future, but because I know he is "The One" with such conviction and certainty, the world cannot and will not tear us apart.

No - he is my world, now. He is my sense of purpose, my guiding light. Every path I have taken has led me to him and now I am no longer lost. Any other path I take, I will always find my way home; to him, my home.

Every idea and inspiration I create in life will now be fueled by him, my muse. I would have never said this about anyone before, but this thought gives me pleasure, now. I am not just living for me anymore but for someone who is an extension of myself, a piece of my soul in another body.

This all sounds so heavy, so serious, and yet our partnership is the complete opposite. It is so free, so comfortable, so natural, so real, so authentic, and so effortless. It just flows and there is no stream I would rather go down. I want to ride his waves for eternity. And, for now, I'll savour the sea I am in. I will swim in bliss and not take a single stroke in his waters for granted.

When I saw him, it was as though all of time stopped so as to focus on the realization that those were the eyes I want to stare into for the rest of my life. His, the last voice I wanted to hear before bed and the voice I wanted to wake to in the morning. His, the body I wanted to be tangled up in mine until we are so old that it aches when we laugh. This was the man I wanted to be *my man*.

I tell him I love him but these three words don't seem like enough. I wish I could create a word to describe just how deeply my soul longs for and adores him. I wish the barriers of language would not limit what should be a boundless expression. I only hope that my eyes speak to him as his do to me. Because that's all I can do; words are messy but my eyes are clear. I want to believe he can read them without limitation, and that they let him know, *"You are safe, you are valued, you are important, you are respected, you are endlessly loved."*

I want to grow old with this man and watch as those eyes stay the same while we, and everything else around us, changes. Those eyes will be my constant. I know this."

I *knew* the Universe recognized that Jordan was the best partner for my life-journey and I *knew* that God wanted us to be together, and Jordan knew the same. The key to moving through the upcoming distance and incoming challenges was to recognize that how this would manifest was not really up to us.

We had no expectations for what "together" ended up looking like. We only knew, and put our energy into knowing, that the end *would be together.* That kind of faith is rewarded, believe me. To trust God with no attachment to the outcome and no definition of how He will create it always comes with beautiful results, but not without a few challenges first.

"I cannot believe I'm living here. I am so in love with you, Paris. I am endlessly grateful that I get to experience this, no matter how long or short it may be. I won't take a second for granted. I will love you as deeply as can for as long as I can. I'll carry with me the memories of you for as long as I live. The imprint you've made on my soul will be part of my legacy.

You have changed me. I am changed. I adore you.

Yet, I cannot funnel all my desire into this one place when so much of the world awaits me.

Paris was the start. Paris was the gas fueling this drive to live my best life. Paris was exactly what I needed, everything I could have ever wanted.

But, what's next?

I'm ready, ready, ready."

- *My personal journal, October 2018*

CHAPTER FIVE
DON'T STOP BELIEVING

One of the many lessons learned over the years that led me to Paris, was to just let things happen how they were meant to unfold. Although I knew I had to leave Jordan - and leave Paris in the process - I had full and complete trust in the Universe that everything on the horizon was for my Highest Good. After all, the Universe hadn't let me down before!

When you are letting go and letting God, it doesn't mean you're not allowed to be sad about your lack of control over the situation, or that you shouldn't have a little bit of anxiety about how it may all fall together in the end. That's perfectly human and completely understandable. However, human emotions which are fear based and stem from the ego are also impermanent and cannot be trusted. Holding onto those emotions and that kind of fear will instigate an attachment to manufactured outcomes and expectations; it's the same thing that causes you to fantasize and build a story in your head about how you wish it will all look in the end. And it's dangerous.

When you are hyper-focusing on a projected reality, you are missing the steps you need to take towards your Highest Good and the true present reality. As I was flying back to Canada and leaving Jordan behind, I could have spent all my hours manufacturing a fearful future in my head where we don't actually end up together and he falls in love with another, but here's what I knew without a doubt:

- I trusted him and his dedication to me, fully, and completely;
- I don't believe in coincidences, only synchronicities, and it was no accident that we met;
- My God wants what is best for me (my Highest Good) and there wasn't a doubt in my mind that that included a life built with Jordan.

If there are doubts that hinder you from releasing expectations and outcomes, you need to figure out the source of those doubts. Do they stem from an intuitive knowing that this, maybe, isn't what you really need (and the fear of that realization)? Do they come from an aspect of your past behaviour that should be unlearned, or an unhealed piece of trauma that would ultimately make you unready for the new chapter in your life? Do they manifest from a space of not truly loving or knowing your worth and would that actually hinder what you are trying to build for yourself?

Uncertainty is never a surprise; fear always has an ultimate source that you can and should pinpoint in order to release, let go and let God. Buddhists are of the belief that it is our attachment to expectations that are the ultimate cause of human suffering. If we are completely open to the path that the Universe lays out to us and trust that, if we walk it with compassion and with an openness to learning and understanding, we will end up in our *nirvana* and we won't have to deal with low-energy feelings such as sadness, pain, or disappointment.

Did I anticipate that my time in Paris would be cut short, right as I was on the precipice of the most beautiful love story of my life? No. Did I know how and where Jordan and I would end up together? Also no. Even so, did I hold onto hope and tell myself, "I know the Universe has big plans for me, so let it all unfold as it must?" *Yes.*

I understand that establishing this trust, especially if life has otherwise been a succession of disappointments, is no easy feat. I'm not asking you to just stick your head under water if you haven't yet learned how to swim, but I can tell you that life is so much easier, more peaceful, stress-free, and joyful if you are unattached to outcomes and narrow down precisely what you can control in a situation (and what requires your active action) and what you have no control over and simply need to let go. When you've mastered the skill of this kind of knowing, life is so much lighter, easier, and smooth sailing.

I still remember a text that Jordan sent me that was actually an indication of how spiritual he really was, showing me how he was mastering this skill, which said, "You and I know the outcome: we are going to be together. No matter what, no matter how it happens. Trust."

Trust.

So I did, and I held onto that as we spent six months across the ocean from each other. And, you know what? It actually wasn't that difficult at all.

TIME WON'T FLY IF YOU DON'T MOVE

One of the most important things I realized while I was waiting for Jordan and I to figure out our future plans together, was how crucial it was to stay busy. Staying busy didn't mean mindlessly "hustling" like I used to do, but instead taking actions that worked towards our goal of being together.

If you have a goal, a plan, a business idea, or a dream, you are doing yourself a disservice by waiting for the "best time" or most comfortable time to take the steps towards it.

Jordan was traveling between interviews and speaking to CEOs in South Africa and beyond, constantly on the move and mentally occupied with all the potential paths available to us and what that would require of him. I was pulled back into an emergency teaching position, working one-on-one with an expelled student in an external (outside of the school) environment. It was definitely the most unexpected and most rewarding experience of my educational career. It also kept me focused on this kid who needed to feel cared for and important, despite his challenging circumstances, and it took my mind off of wallowing over the time Jordan and I were spending apart and playing the victim.

I viewed each hour at work as an hour bringing me

THE TRANSFORMATIONAL PATH

closer to a life with Jordan again. I viewed each dollar I made as a way to fund our reunion. I was working on making our long-distance a short-distance through each of my daily actions, and Jordan was too.

I wouldn't call it *distraction* because distractions are used as escapism and we live in this world so we must not try to escape it; we must adapt to it, learn from it, heal within it, and accept it as it is. I didn't want to escape my reality because Jordan was a part of it - no matter how many miles there were between us. I wanted to *make* my reality and *form it* to look how I felt it best suited us both.

I was manufacturing our future through my active participation in life, rather than staying under the sheets, crying about distance, and being depressed. I was acting in a way so that, if tomorrow would be the day we would have to make a decision, I would be ready for it.

Oftentimes, a difficult situation or a challenge will prevent you from having the strength to move forward. This also rings true for things like following your dreams; the internalized fear makes you believe in millions of excuses that stop you from actually taking the next step towards that goal. We can even try to convince ourselves that we will, "do it when the time feels right."

This leaves us in a constant limbo and stagnant space, always looking for the next excuse to hold off on actually making moves.

If you are waiting for a sign from the Universe to make a move, I am sure you've already missed it. The Universe wants us to succeed and wants us to take concrete actions towards a purposeful life that is well lived. The longer you wait for the "perfect time," the more hidden it becomes. This is because each hesitancy to step forward is actually a step back.

So, I was keeping myself occupied and consciously performing each action with not only gratitude to the Universe at what awaited me at the end of the tunnel, but by being aware of how it would benefit our journey together in the future.

LONG DISTANCE IS EASY (WITH THE RIGHT PARTNER AND COMPROMISE)

If you had asked me pre-Paris if I could ever be okay with the idea of a long-distance relationship, I would have laughed in your face. I was incapable of imagining something like that working for a few reasons:

- I didn't have that kind of commitment to anyone and knew my connection would wane quite quickly
- I didn't trust any of my previous partners (and none of them provided a security that enabled me to trust them)

- I had the "independent woman" mindset and integrated it as an essential part of my identity

For some reason, in North America in particular, there is a mentality that is fed into young women that they *need no man* (or partner), that they don't need to commit because life is short, and that being desired adds to your self-worth.

You can ask anyone who knew me and they will tell you that I was certainly a selfie queen at one point in time. I really did validate my importance based upon how many "likes" a sexy photo got. I know many people who will say, "If you're feeling yourself, then why not just post the sexy selfie!? Throw the whole man out if he tries to stop you!"

However, after I committed myself completely to Jordan, I got very honest with myself:

- Were these photos really for me or for external attention?
- Did I need to show the public these photos when I could get validation from the source that truly matters (by sending them directly to Jordan)?
- What did I gain by being desired by men other than my boyfriend?
- How could this hurt Jordan, even indirectly?

- Most importantly, I approached this from a more spiritual perspective;
- What did these photos add to my spiritual growth?
- Does Spirit truly care how sexy I look?
- How does feeling sexy benefit my Ascension?
- How does this align with my practice and what is it teaching others who are learning from me?

There is a reason why Yogis in India and Buddhists in Tibet all wear uniform and tattered clothing; the body is temporal and unimportant, and seeking uniqueness amongst your community simply leads to challenges and suffering. When the focus is put on the spirit instead of the sexy clothes you're wearing, your priorities are clearly defined with God and you no longer risk the temptations of the ego.

That being said, I'm not asking you to consider dressing like a nun or adorn a hijab as necessary to stay humble. You were still given this body in this earthly existence to fully enjoy and embrace it, but reconsider the necessity of social media validation and how it may, actually, indirectly impact your partner that you are committed to. What does it tell them if you seek approval and desire outside of the relationship?

Because, come on, is that bathing suit butt shot *really* for you?

Be honest with yourself.

Knowing the distance between me and Jordan was going to increase - the desire we had for one another and the disappointment in the lack of physical content - for me to continue to post these selfies and cater to the gaze of other men and women on social media would have been disrespectful to him. I respected him more than I *needed* to post my sexy outfit on social media.

This was a compromise I wouldn't have considered with relationships in the past because, quite honestly, the same level of respect wasn't there. Jordan showed and expressed to me his utmost trust and respect for me, and emphasized that there was absolutely no jealousy that existed in this relationship together; he knew our connection was Divine, infallible, and would not have anyone come between it. I felt the same with regard to him, no matter the distance between the two of us.

Instead of just thinking about myself when on social media, I put how this would impact him as first in my mind. This, I believe, is necessary for a truly healthy relationship. In addition to this very minor compromise, I also took a very good look at my friendships with the opposite sex and whether I was maintaining connections with people who would hurt Jordan, who had expressed interest in me as more than a friend or who did not look at my new relationship as permanent but fleeting.

By looking at these "friendships" with a more honest lens, it was easy to see who I was keeping around for further validation of my desirability and who were real, honest, platonic friends. And, from there, I was able to weed out the men who merely wanted me, wanted me to be miserable like them or did not view my relationship with Jordan as very serious. I ended those friendships with very honest declarations where I let them know that I did not feel that our friendship aligned in a harmonious way with my new commitment in my life, or I did not feel that our friendship valued the importance of Jordan in my life.

This is not to say that I don't believe men and women can be friends. On the contrary, I believe that platonic friendships that balance both the feminine and masculine are essential to growth. Nevertheless, I do think it's important to assess which friendships are "fair" for your partner, and whether you are holding onto some connections for the wrong reasons rather than genuine connection and community growth.

For example, I was trying to maintain a friendship with my ex from a relationship of four years, only to discover that any discussion of Jordan led him to change the topic. When I asked him about this, he said he found it difficult to be happy for me when hearing about a new relationship. We had been separated for three years at this point and he had other relationships since then. I told him that Jordan was a primary figure in my life now and wouldn't be going away. It would be have been unfair to continue a friendship with this ex when something that is central to my overall life growth was being ignored or dismissed.

On the other hand, an old ex-turned-friend of mine was very excited that I found my soulmate and was very eager to meet him. This is why I emphasize that not *all* friendships with the opposite sex are inappropriate, but you need to honestly assess whether some of them hurt, hinder, or otherwise do not benefit your newly established partnership.

This was only something that I really needed to work on in the relationship because Jordan (and French people in general) did not form close friendships with the opposite sex, other than the partners of his close male friends. It was not something he asked of me but something I considered with honesty because of how important he was to me. I knew if roles were reversed, he would have done the same.

It's important to distinguish that you should not *change* for a partner and your partner should not expect you to change. Your interests, your characteristics, and your entire Self should be loved and accepted without conditions. If you were a vegetarian when you met your partner, your partner should not pressure you to eat meat. If you really loved watching reality television before meeting your partner, your partner should not belittle your interests. If you have a passion for creative arts before your partner, they should not push you to drop this passion.

Yet, in order for a relationship to succeed, you need to be able to compromise for the partnership.

Drop the "independent" act and don't downplay the importance of your partner in your life path. Ensure they feel valued and respected (and vice versa) through eliminated learned behaviours that offer no long-term benefit to a healthy partnership. Ask them what makes them comfortable and uncomfortable early on, and come to an understanding about what to compromise on. Jordan never asked anything of me, but through my dedication to him, I was able to look at things through a more honest lens and narrow down what was not central to my identity and hindered our growth.

My relationship with Jordan also introduced me to Love Languages[1]. Sometimes, when we are in a partnership with someone, we show them love, attention, and affection in the ways that *we* want to be shown love, attention, and affection. We express our commitment to one other by loving them the way we want to be loved ourselves. I quickly discovered that for relationships to be successful, we need to learn how others like to have love expressed to them and to make an effort - even if it's out of our comfort zone - to demonstrate it to them in that manner.

My Love Language is verbal and words of affection. As an Aquarius - and Jordan being the same - communication is central to bonding with people I care about and maintaining a healthy relationship. As such, I emphasized to Jordan how I would truly *need this* during our time apart. This agreement also made the transition into long-distance a much easier one.

We made sure to set aside time for us to video chat at least once every day, despite our timezone differences. Even if something would arise that wouldn't allow me or Jordan to make it to our "video call date," we expressed it ahead of time so we didn't keep the other person waiting. We made an effort to put aside time for one another, no matter the circumstances.

It is very easy to get sucked back into the familiar lifestyle from before a partner when you are separated, and one of the grounds for success, regardless of your Sun Sign, is to make communication the foundation upon which you build your relationship.

A famous German philosopher, Friedrich Nietzsche, said that you should never marry someone you can't talk to, because that's all you'll have when you grow old. Looks fade, physical desire quells, adventuring calms down, and before long you're aged and sitting next to one another on a bench for hours at a time - all you will have is your conversation.

When you work to build a relationship upon the foundations of communication, which is beneficial to your mental, emotional, and spiritual health, you are creating a base that is rock solid and transcends attachment to solely earthly pleasure. Desire is not a bad thing (it's human, after all), but attachment to desire is where you can cross into more dangerous territory. So, bonds built upon talking and exposing our souls to one another, daily, truly helps solidify the Divinity of that bond.

Another lesson learned through time apart from Jordan, was that if I wanted this partner to be an equal in my life and the soulmate that lead me further down the path to betterment and spiritual growth, putting myself first would not lead to our success as a couple. From following my dreams to Paris, I had learned the importance of making myself a priority when I otherwise spent a life serving the ideals of others. Now, I was bringing someone into my life and that forced me to re-evaluate my strategy.

If you want to build a life with your equal, there are sacrifices involved in the process. I had lived my dream and now I needed to give Jordan the space to make a career and life decision that would allow him to experience the same kind of abundant bliss that I felt by moving to Paris.

Sometimes the sacrifice means that we follow our partners in directions we wouldn't have anticipated, other times it may mean that we need to put our work on hold. For me and Jordan, I had to re-evaluate what was most important for us to build our lives together most successfully.

Following my educational fill-in with the expelled student, I received a promotion to Special Education Administrator. This meant a great job title and leadership role, a monetary increase in my already impressive salary, and a secure transition into the high school sector. In addition to that, I had a basement apartment at my parents' place which meant I wasn't paying rent and was pocketing everything I was making. This would have been a pretty great situation for Jordan to step into, but a visa into Canada and securing a job there was proving to be far from easy. Furthermore, I knew that education was no longer meant to be a part of my path, so would this new commitment just make me miserable over time?

On the other hand, Jordan was looking at opportunities in South Africa where I wasn't comfortable on moving to, but I was willing to "try it" on the basis of him reassuring me it, "wasn't for forever."

Securing a visa would be far easier for me, but it would mean I couldn't work for a bit. Jordan had to be okay with supporting me if this was the case and he was comfortable with that possibility.

I truly believe it was both of our "openness to everything" attitudes and our trust that the Universe would find us something to reunite that allowed us to come together again in only six months - and come together in a completely unexpected but absolutely perfect city, at that.

THE UNIVERSE IS FUNNY SOMETIMES

One evening, during one of our nightly video chats, Jordan told me he secured a position for a company and he was ready to accept it if I was willing to jump on board with the plan. He wanted to confirm with me first before taking the leap because he knew it would involve sacrifice on my behalf and he told me he was willing to say no if it was asking too much of me.

I asked him where we were headed and he told me... *Strasbourg.*

I had never heard of Strasbourg before. It sounded German and I wondered about my visa, but it turned out to be in France. This meant that renewing the Work/Holiday visa I first came to France with would be an absolute breeze. Thank you, Universe!

However, that's not the funny part... as a child who always had her nose deep within the pages of a book, it was obvious that my favourite Disney princess would be Belle from Beauty and the Beast. Library loving, tough girl Belle - who didn't need no man! - was an idol. In fact, when dreaming of Paris, I would often post photos of her on social media that said, "I want much more than this provincial life!"

My Strasbourg story is truly proof that God listens to every soul-calling and every dream you wish to manifest than sits in your heart, the key is to simply not get attached to how or when that dream will come to fruition. Belle is from the Strasbourg region of France - Alsace.

Yes, I would be living in the literal region of Belle, with colourful buildings that looked like they were plucked out of this Disney movie. And, although I told Jordan that I had never heard about Alsace before he told me about his job offer, that was incorrect.

In 2018, before moving to Paris, I went to my spiritual advisor, Carol Righton, at Akasha's Den in Oakville (my home away from home - best esoteric store in the *world*), to ask her about this transition and what I should know about the journey I was making. Not only did she tell me that I would meet a tall, dark, and handsome Frenchman during this trip - which I "poo-pooed" during our conversation - she also told me that I should open myself up beyond Paris because she saw me in a place called, "A-ahl-Alsiss? Alsass? Search for it."

Again, I went there to talk about Paris so I "poo-pooed" this comment (and didn't find anything when I searched for the region phonetically) so it slipped my mind until a few days after that 2019 video chat call with Jordan. The Universe is funny sometimes!

Since I didn't have an attachment to where me and Jordan would begin to build our life together, and since I motioned to the Universe that I was willing and accepting of this union being on God's terms and not my own, they gifted me Strasbourg. This was a city that I dreamt of living in as a young girl, that would allow me to release attachment to solely Paris, and which would be the easiest option for our reunion (based on visas and work for everyone involved). I made Jordan a priority, I trusted God completely, and I was given a new but easy path to traverse. Not to mention, Strasbourg was perfect. Truly perfect.

This would not be the last time that the Universe would manifest me exactly what I hoped for in passing and released attachment to, and that seems to be the real key to the Law of Attraction. You don't need to write it down a million times, you don't need to think about it every minute of every day, you don't need to put a post-it on your mirror to remind you of what you want. You just need to say it, write it once, or speak it to the Universe with heart-felt intention, already existing gratitude, and then release all expectations of how it will show itself.

No timelines, no fantasy-building in your head, no anger, or impatience with how long it is taking, just a security and trust in God.

Once the seed that you planted in your heart has been left to grow on its own accord, that's when it sprouts! And, that's when you're reminded, "Hey, this is exactly what I hoped for! God listens, trust me."

The Law of Attraction tries to tell you that God needs constant reminding, but that just shows the Universe that you don't trust in it's method, that you are far too attached to everything looking and being as you expect it to, or that you want control in all situations.

Manifesting is not about control at all; it's about release and putting the work into what *can* be controlled. In my case, it was just focusing on the other aspects of my journey (researching how to obtain my visa, packing accordingly, saving money to buy my flight, etc.) and trusting that the path to these particular aspects of my soul-longing would reveal themselves when I was ready to tread them.

So, I packed my things (and my dog) and moved over to Strasbourg to join my darling Jordan in the newest chapter of our life. I actually liked that we were beginning outside of Paris because he, having been a born and raised Parisian, was ready to distance himself from the city and I didn't want to come to resent it after it had provided me with so many lessons and so much joy. Jordan had family in Alsace and his mother was born in Alsace (funny how life always goes in a full circle) but this was going to be a new experience for the both of us.

We quickly found *home* in Strasbourg.

It was beyond perfect - not to mention affordable - and that affordability allowed me to dip my toes into new work ventures. I was teaching English after school for a salary that would no longer have me sitting in the red, but I was also feeling a call back to my written spiritual work which, at the time, was written tarot readings. After putting this side business on pause for four years, I, once again, had a night-time dream that encouraged me to revive my practice. Of course, by this point I had learned that I absolutely cannot ignore my guides speaking to me through my dreams and needed to just jump in - *so I did*.

I had built up a small but significant mailing list off my apprentice and donation-based clients and sent off a message that "Seeking Celestial Grace" was coming back to serve those needing guidance, on a part-time basis. This allowed me to cater to two of my known soul callings: writing (since my material is presented to clients in written format) and healing. Now that I was living a secure and joyous life that many people would dream of, I thought it was important to help others also find that abundance.

SELFLESS WORK LEADS TO REWARD

God rewards those who do selfless work, but there is something very important that is often missed; you cannot do completely selfless work for others without having first spent time healing and aligning yourself. You can, in fact, do damage to the paths that souls are walking if you attempt to guide and direct them when you are misaligned, lost, dealing with trauma, or living in chaos. In fact, I think it is exceptionally dangerous (and frankly selfish) to practice spiritual healing and guidance work, or even offer yourself up to lost souls seeking your assistance, without being in a centered and stable space yourself.

The battle of depression, anxiety, and PTSD is something that is ongoing for the rest of your life. You can stop having episodes, but you never stop managing and working on your healing so that you don't return to that space again. I have, unfortunately, seen the romanticization of mental illness on social media; it is sold to people scrolling as a "normal state" and presented in a way that makes people believe that not having mental illness makes you boring.

Mental illness is not a normal spiritual state to be situated in!

If that was the case, people would go on year-long spiritual journeys searching for their ideal mental illness.

It is a chaotic and unbalanced place to be in - I know - and the peaceful life that follows intense medical and spiritual intervention is unmatched.

It makes sense that I put my business on pause for four years as I went through intense healing journeys, unlearning adventures, and self-discovery pathways; I was in no place to guide others while I was going through all these profound changes. If I didn't have my life and my trauma figured out, how could I possibly provide any valuable guidance to someone else? If I wasn't listening to my guides and angelic team about what I needed, how could I possibly hear what they had to say about someone else's journey?

That is not to say that the best mentors are perfect or have achieved enlightenment, but they should have a comfortable grasp on their traumas and triggers. They need to be *regulated* emotionally, mentally, and spiritually in order to safely guide their flock. Even Jesus had moments of emotional outbursts, confusion, and discomfort but he was still an Ascended shepherd of men; he just knew when he was unable to commit to his healer duties and, in fact, took a very large "sabbatical" between preaching as a child to rabbis and coming back to Israel to really lead with his message.

When we moved to Strasbourg, my own sabbatical ended. I was in a really steady place and was continuing to live the life of my dreams, so I wanted to share that joy and abundance with others. As such, I decided to step back into spiritual work. I truly believe that choosing to share this state of gratitude with others was rewarded by the Universe because I had an unexpected influx of spiritual clients right after re-launching.

I do trust that God rewards people who do not hoard their happiness, who do not form a hyper-fixated attachment on abundance being limited and exclusive for some but not all.

Abundance is available to *everyone*. It is not limited in production and is not exclusive to the "more gifted." It doesn't matter where you are on your journey, so long as you are willing to put in the work to heal and Ascend, you'll be rewarded for it emotionally, mentally, physically, spiritually, and financially! I wanted this avenue of wisdom to be open to my clients.

My spiritual work went so well that I was able to take it from a part-time passion project to a full-time gig. So now, not only was I writing on the daily (a soul-calling that I knew I had to make time for), I was also able to dedicate extra hours in my schedule to helping others also follow their life purpose and inner calling to abundance. The financial compensation that I was getting from this spiritual freelancing was comparable to what I was making in Canada as a teacher, but for less work hours in the day - something I am sure that many people would have found hard to believe.

Eventually, Jordan received an unexpected promotion and we were packing up our bags and getting ready to move yet again - back to Paris, no less! It seemed to be that my chapter there wasn't over and there was more to be learned.

I decided the move back to Paris and my constant pull *away* from teaching meant that it was time for me to end that part of my journey fully and completely. I made the decision to focus all my attention on my spiritual business and to dip my toes into freelance writing, since I had a passion for language that needed to be satiated. I believe the decision to stick to *my path* without hesitation and to break free of the confines of that milestone accomplishment I carried over with me from Canada (being an educator) were also rewarded by the Universe.

My workdays had schedules that were set by me. I was able to take breaks when I wanted and go out with friends when I decided I needed a break. I was able to take days off without being questioned about my reason for "skipping" and being asked to make plans for any person filling in for me. I was working from home and in a space I created just for me. I wasn't ending my day with emotional, mental, spiritual, or physical exhaustion. I loved what I was doing, I was happy doing it, and I was no longer under the microscopic eye of being "a teacher with a social media presence."

Most importantly, those Monday Scaries that people

have on Sundays didn't exist for me anymore. You know you're following the right path when work no longer feels like work. It was pure magic!

On top of all that, I was providing significant income to the household. I was even gifted a dream about a beginner's tarot deck that I was told by my angelic team that I *had* to create. When I did, it had a successful Kickstarter crowd-funding campaign, raising over 13 thousand Euros to bring it to life. This "kick-started" the creation of multiple decks that are now loved around the world.

I saw my path, I walked my path, I was sharing the abundance of my path with others, and I was being rewarded for my dedication. God is good!

AN OPENNESS TO EVERYTHING

As expected, transitioning back into France resulted in many hoops to leap through, exhausting paperwork to fill out, and learning what it means to be patient. Living in France long-term is not like being in France as a tourist or on a temporary visa. Just when you believe you've finished a giant file of paperwork, the bureaucracy asks you for more documents or says they're missing documents that you've already included (and you now need to convince them that they just missed it, when they have no desire to look at your file again). This chaos completely changed my perspective on stress.

My new mentality: when a challenge is presented to me or a roadblock appears in my life to make things more difficult for me, I need to ask myself - is this something I have control over? If I do, what steps can I begin to implement to start making the situation less stressful for me? If I don't have control over this situation, how is stress truly beneficial to it? It's not and the situation is out of my hands, so it's time to release any stress or frustration with a big, deep breath.

For example, it took three months for the French administration to look at my residency application and then, within seconds, it was declined on the basis of one missing document? Okay, add the document, wait again, no big deal....

Another example was when my package was lost by the post, even though they gave me a slip to pick up the package, but now cannot seem to find where it disappeared to? Okay, nothing can be done... Deep breath, message the seller with the issue, hope for a return, and *release*.

This mentality made living in France much easier to deal with (I still use these coping mechanisms today). It's actually a very spiritual way to approach all problems in your life because it instills a mindset of non-attachment to not only the cause of the stress but also how it may all work out for you (or not) in the end. Sometimes things will not play out as you hoped and you need to learn to cope with that in a way that does not add layers of frustration and exhaustion to your life, but that makes life easier for you.

The beauty that comes with this mentality of ease and flow, is the fact it brings a lot of joy and profound change into your life. This is the ultimate key to manifestation - working and moving and taking action in your life, but without expectation to outcome and with non-attachment to the stress that comes from roadblocks.

Over the next few years, I grew within the marketing and advertising industry and had more freelance writing opportunities presented to me. I graduated with a Masters in Library and Information Studies a year before most of my peers, even though I had taken a sabbatical for my mental health back in 2017.

Jordan proposed to me on the one year anniversary of our meeting and we were married in a very small Town Hall ceremony seven months later (a lesson on stress release as COVID prevented my family from being present during my marriage).

My spiritual gifts continued to grow as I continued to work with others, making my clairaudient mediumship abilities much stronger. This allowed me to slowly eliminate tarot readings from my services and delve into direct spirit channeling and communication, as well as spiritual counseling.

Shortly after our three year "meeting anniversary," we were surprised with the news that I was pregnant. (More on the heavy healing work that came forward before and after motherhood in later chapters.)

Jordan was given numerous promotions to choose from, enabling us to select the ideal place to move to and begin a new chapter for our son who was on the way. He took a promotion in Geneva, Switzerland, which allowed us to move to Saint Jorioz, France. Saint Jorioz is just 10 km from Annecy and, in 2018, before meeting Jordan, I wrote this in my journal after visiting Annecy on my own:

"I loved Annecy. I wish I had at least two more days there to see more neighbouring towns and climb more mountains. In all honesty, I could picture myself living in Annecy. I liked that it had city access but a small-town feel. I liked the intimacy of the city and the kindness of the people. And, most of all, I loved the mountains and the water.

Paris is the first of its kind in that I'm not normally a "city girl". I find a small cabin in the woods idea very appealing. Paris is the only city that tugged at my heartstrings when I am normally drawn to quieter places with more nature. My father was born in a region that is literally called 'the foot of the mountain' and my adoration of bodies of water has been a part of me for as long as I can remember. When a city/town has mountains and water, to me, that's perfection. That is as good as it gets. That beats any city, any day. And so it makes sense that I am drawn to a place like this."

In addition, before I was pregnant and before Jordan was given his choice of city to move to for work, my spiritual advisor, Carol, told me: "I see Jordan working in Switzerland, but I see you living in France. You're standing in your backyard, looking at the mountains, and holding a little boy."

Just six months later, we discovered Jordan's promotion and my pregnancy in the same week. Not far after that, I discovered I was carrying a little boy. And I can see the mountains from my backyard.

Remember, there are no coincidences in life; God hears every wish in your heart and will present it to you when it's the perfect moment, when you are absolutely ready for it. Even if it is just said in passing - especially if it is just said in passing - but if the Universe knows it will lead to your growth and betterment, you can be sure it will someway and somehow appear in your life.

Once you stop playing God and, instead, let the Universe take control of the wheel - while still being an active participant on the clutch, signals, and dials - magic seems to unfold even better than you anticipated. The roads you will be brought down, will transform you.

---

1. Chapman, D.G. (2014). *The 5 Love Languages.* Moody Publishers.

"The Spiritual Path can only be traveled through the daily experience of love."

- Paulo Coelho

CHAPTER SIX
SPIRITUAL LESSONS AND CHANNELED DOWNLOADS

I don't know if my love for Jordan and the joy of the beautiful life we were building together was the catalyst of my spiritual gifts being amplified - the reason for a re-Awakening of my connection to the Divine - or if it was just being in a state of joy from my move back in 2018 that allowed me to reach a very centered and content state, which subsequently lead to my heart opening. I do know that an alignment to the energy of Love, which is God's energy, is essential to traversing a spiritual path more confidently, securely, and quickly. It's hard to avoid aligning with energy when you are cultivating a life that is founded upon such a Divine and beautiful love!

THE TRANSFORMATIONAL PATH

All I know is that I was doing work that was not only more impactful for my clients but was also more profound and meaningful for my own life. My spiritual advisor Carol gave me the title of "Wisdom Writer" since she said that writing was my access point to Universal Energy. I hear, I know, I feel, I transmute through text. She helped me formulate this description of my work:

> I go into the origin of your soul and theorize the lessons presented to me, for you to gain the Awareness necessary to make a change or manifest the Earthly experience that you desire. I have access to your Soul's Blueprint and have the opportunity to present the path of healing to you. I move through every level of communication in the Angelic Realm and my mediumship contains subconscious Reiki healing by transmuting the finite into unity with the Divine.

My gifts have always been a part of my life. As a young child, I was far more clairvoyant (clear-seeing) than I am now. I have very clear recollections about out of body experiences at night and seeing earth creatures such as fairies and gnomes. I would also have very vivid dreams about the future and vocalize these "predictions" to others, primarily adults, who would roll their eyes or look at me weirdly. This dismissal caused me to ask for my gifts to be shut off; your guides will listen to you if this is truly what you want.

At twelve years old, I was given my first set of tarot cards from my mother. I became known amongst my friends as the "tarot reader" and was often asked to bring the cards with me to sleepovers. Tarot, from twelve years old and onwards, continued to be an active part of my life, becoming even more prominent when I had my - what I like to call - spiritual RE-Awakening at around 24 years old.

Spirituality became a far more active part of my life during this time and my tarot readings became a gift I would share with others online. In addition, I could literally *feel* my connection with my angelic team and guides start to grow stronger. My predictive or spiritually insightful dreams began to come back to me, and I was dedicating a lot of time to healing in order to grow.

This was the *big key* to developing my gifts. I needed to heal a lot of my earthly trauma from both this life and my past lives, which I carried over into this life. This all happened as I was coming to terms with my sexual assault, so a lot of my healing was medical - therapy, counseling, and even some medication. With each barrier I leaped over in my healing journey, I could feel the connection grow and I could feel the inclination towards living a life more aligned with my spiritual path start to strengthen.

Having always been a writer at heart, I funneled my spiritual gifts into text. I would write out tarot readings for my clients and friends rather than speaking to them, I would write spiritual blog posts, and I would journal in a way that was very much like an open release of my spirit.

I was not an auditory learner. I chose to skip university lectures because I couldn't process them. I need to watch television shows and movies with subtitles on. And so, the irony of having clairaudient gifts is not lost on me! Yet, the Universe was just teaching me to listen deeply and it gave me writing - my talent - as a way to transmute my gifts into something life-changing for others.

My clairaudient gifts were first made aware to me when I was alone in Rocamadour, France. I had my first channeling experience where I was not only informed of my clairaudient abilities - a gift I wasn't even fully aware of possessing - but also told about my life's purpose of writing. As such, over time, I began to compile lessons that came to me as "informed lessons" through my spiritual journaling, but also through channeled experiences of connecting to my guides, the Angelic plane, or Ascended Masters.

SPIRITUAL LESSONS AND CHANNELED DOWNLOADS

This chapter is a compilation of those spiritual life lessons and channeled dialogues, which I feel will help you better navigate a Divinely manifested and abundant life, beginning with the first download I ever received.

It is truly important that I stress that this gift is not unique to me; everyone has a connection to Source and everyone has one avenue that is stronger than the rest. It is simply a matter of practice, training, routine, worship and, most importantly, healing, that helps develop and strengthen that connection, much like a muscle. In addition, every time these lessons or channeled dialogues are gifted to me, they are done so without emotional reaction.

I caution that anyone who begins to flex their connection muscle be aware of feeling overly scared or excited. This is usually a sign of either a dialogue with your ego or with lower energetic points of contact. After a bit of reflection on the messages you receive, you may analyze it with your human side and have a *feeling* towards it, but at the point of connection, you should feel very energetically neutral to ensure it is Divine in the first place.

THE BLACK MADONNA - ROCAMADOUR, SEPTEMBER 1ST 2018

The following message was handwritten in a notebook and gifted to me directly from the Black Madonna as I sat in the church in Rocamadour, France. It began as I was watching a wailing woman in the church who kept pushing her child away from her, when she wanted to join her in prayer.

"When you pray in public, do not moan for me or rock for all to see, do not make a show of this private act. I am listening. You needn't move and I still hear your heart. I am in your heart. I listen to the secret prayers of your heart. The rocking does not appease me. It disappoints me.

You are made in my image, you are sacred, you do not need to act lesser than. We are one. I am you – you are me. We are one. Do well to know this. And do well to treat yourself as sacred. You are not an object of sin, you are a beacon of light and sacred potential. Do not let the church convince you otherwise. Everything I am, you are too.

You are holy. You are blessed. You are a saint. We are one. I love you and I am with you always because we are one. Goddess, Queen, Sacred Being. So I am, so too you are.

Go and tell the world of this. Go and guide the nations to light. I am with you. I am with you. Be my mouth. Write for all. Convert many.

Be blessed.

Live for me and my Son. Live for light and grace and live for truth. Write for me. Do you accept?

Then it is. So it is, so it is, so it is.

You will write and change lives.

Your purpose is to write for me. Be my mouth.

When you write they who read will listen.

You are a living dream come true and your journey inspires others to hear you and follow suite."

At this point, the child of the woman went to sit beside her mom and the mom got up and went to another pew to pray away from the child.

"What this woman is doing hurts me – isolating the child – she holds darkness. The child is light.

She is Spirit. The child finds comfort in me. I am with her.

Say it. Say that I speak to you the way [Archangel] Michael does. Say it everywhere."

At this point, I did communicate to Madonna that this responsibility makes me fearful of condemnation, isolation, or ridicule.

"So am I. Scared of isolation? But I am with you. So you are never alone. Do not forget.

I do not care about the rosary. Speak from your heart with passion and the Gods will hear you.

Devotion is not decided by an institution but by a person themselves, it is not taught or passed down, but experienced in a moment of surrealism and earthly wonder.

You will move mountains and I am with you, always.

We are one.

We are one.

We are one.

Always.

Light above all.

> Speak truth.
> Write truth."

PAST LIVES AND REINCARNATION

I'd like to speak to this concept as there have been numerous references to it throughout my text and it is likely to be touched upon in later this chapter, as well.

As souls on the other side, we choose to enter into earthly life experiences and learn specific lessons. These lessons are often guided by karmic ties from previous lives, but are generally geared towards ultimate soul expansion. Our angelic team and God him/her/itself want us to break out of this cycle through Ascension, but sometimes there are a few more steps we need to take before we get there. So, we choose to go through the process of reincarnation.

All of us, every single soul on earth, have had numerous (nearing the hundreds) of life experiences. Ascended Masters, for example, are individuals who have had numerous soul experiences and, in their last earthly life, Ascended with an agreement to be a guide for others due to the life they lived on earth (eg. Mother Mary, Jesus, Saint Germain, etc.). Often, the struggles that we go through in our earthly life are actually struggles we have been through before, and we are being tested to see if we traverse through it differently - meaning we actually are able to learn the lesson in this lifetime and let go of that struggle for future reincarnations.

It is also possible that many of the unexplained fears that we carry into this lifetime are heavily influenced by traumatic memories that are embedded in our spirit from our past lives. For example, an irrational fear of water could be related to death by drowning in a past life, or an inability to advocate to yourself could be related to being punished in a past life for speaking your truth. If there is no present-life trauma associated with these life challenges, it is likely due to past life traumas.

I experienced this in my own life. I had an absolutely unexplainable fear of motherhood and having children. Everything about the idea made me terrified. I saw no appeal in it, no draw to the cuteness of babies, and no desire to continue my lineage. When I began dating Jordan, he did express that he wished to have children with me. I told him I would give him a child, but he needed to give me time to overcome this fear and be okay with the idea of being pregnant and giving birth, and that I did not know how long that would take.

One day, I came across the works of Dr. Brian Weiss[1], a hypnotist who discovered he could access the past lives of his clients through regression therapy and help them heal many of the irrational traumas, fears, and even unexplained illnesses (like asthma) that were carried over from other lifetimes. While his guided meditations never seemed to pull me into the regression state, I knew that, with my excellent relationship with my guides and angelic team, I could ask for the same kind of healing as I slept. Since dreams are a primary access source for a lot of my communication with my team, I would ask for healing at night.

Over the span of a month, I had numerous past life regressions as I slept. I knew they were not dreams because they *felt* like a memory but didn't feature me, as I am now in this lifetime. In each one, there was a realization of the source of the trauma and a deep request for forgiveness by my spirit. Though I don't remember all of these regressions, two in particular still stick out to me.

In one, I was a new mother and my child died shortly after childbirth. It was tremendously heartbreaking, and I felt the emptiness and loss of this soul memory. When I woke up from the experience, my fear of raising children vanished and the idea of, "They will be safe with me," replaced it. In another, I was a young girl who was sexually assaulted and had a baby as a result of this assault. I was very, very young, and was, of course, in no way ready to parent a child when I was a child myself. So, I neglected the baby and let them cry until they died of starvation in their crib. I was then persecuted by the women around me for my cruelty.

When I came to the realization of what I was witnessing in this regression, I asked the baby to please forgive me and told the spirit that I was sorry that I didn't allow it a chance at life. At this point, I woke up from the regression and saw Archangel Michael appear in my bedroom and lift the spirit of this baby out of me, indicating that our karmic ties were now released. I burst into tears, and simultaneously felt an immense weight lift off of me. That regression was the final key to eliminating all the fear I had towards pregnancy, motherhood, and children. I literally told Jordan that I was no longer afraid, and it was true. It was completely gone.

Shortly after this experience, without planning or intention, I began to dream about holding a child in my arms. One night, I had repeated dreams about performing a pregnancy test and seeing "positive" on the test. I woke up that morning and decided to just take the test; it showed *pregnant* within seconds on the screen. I burst into tears of joy as I showed Jordan and, truly, this regression healing I went through lasted through my entire pregnancy. There was not a single moment of fear or uncertainty that infiltrated my experience - and I believe this is what made my pregnancy a symptom-free joy.

I do believe that in our lives, we reincarnate with many of the same spirits to re-learn unlearned lessons. These are our soulmates. I also think that we are meant to connect with one soul in particular, our Divine Soulmate, that is meant to show us a compassion that leads us to personal betterment and fast-tracks us to Ascension (if we are able to enter the relationship as healthy and healed people). In addition, we may encounter Twin Flames who are spirits we have a history with which rush into our lives with a lot of passion and teach us an extremely harsh and painful lesson. It is often difficult to disconnect from Twin Flames which is why they return in so many lives, and why people so often mix them up with real love; there is a familiarity about them, including the pain they cause us. However, they're not meant to be a long-lasting presence in our lives.

I do believe that my mother was my child in a past life and this is why I don't have enough patience with her when she is emotional or hyper-sensitive, and why I always saw her in more of a "cute" lens than a "authority" lens. I also believe my husband's sister may have been his mother and his wife in a past life, which explains her possessiveness and need to control him in this life. Spirits make agreements to return in various formats depending on the lifetime and the lesson needing to be learned.

I am also under the belief - and have had it confirmed

by my spiritual team - that, as souls deciding to return, we do agree to many of the lessons we are set to learn in this lifetime beforehand. This further emphasizes the saying, "God will never give you anything you can't handle," because you actually agreed to handle it before entering into this lifetime! Of course, being human with limited awareness, many people fall from the path of learning that they agreed to traverse before reincarnation, and so they are meant to repeat it all again in the next round.

Of course, the cycle of reincarnation can stop once Ascension is reached. The Buddhists call it Nirvana and the Christians call it heaven; there is an "endpoint" when a soul has learned all the lessons it needs to know, has cut the karmic ties that continue to follow them in lifetimes, and has lived a compassionate and selfless life dedicated to the betterment of others. Eventually, souls can reach a point where they are asked by their team, "Do you wish to continue the earthly experience or become a guide to other earthly souls?"

Your team of spirit guides is made up of individuals who have lived full and complete earthly lives and have numerous lives and lessons which help make them so wise, and now they've taken up the assignment of helping *you* be the best person you could be.

ARCHANGEL MICHAEL - DOWNLOAD ON MANIFESTING

"I am who you call Michael, though, to me, I am Mik-ael. "Like God," I am not though. I am for righteousness of the same caliber. I emanate love and look to protect those who seek my loyalty and friendship. I will not appear on my own accord; I require your call. An act of humility which in turn begins an ascension into grace and protection. The Free Will of man is not as complex as they may believe. The power that they have when they just ask is enormous! So many missed opportunities as they sit in their sadness and wallow in their inactions.

Mani-festus – it is in their hands and the Kingdom of Heaven is in their grasp. I speak not of a place but of a state. They seek fulfillment outside themselves when it is in them all along.

You are loved. Fame is Nothing. I am near."

I really appreciated that Archangel Michael referenced the Latin roots of manifest: to grab with your hands, to not sit stagnant and wait for an opportunity to present itself to you. Being sad and suffering is a really - surprisingly - comfortable state to be in, and the work required to move through it is extensive. Yet, at the same time, it's just a single step out of your reach!

Just get up and the Universe recognizes this as enough.

MASTERY OF SELF - A CHANNEL FROM A HIGHER GUIDE

"The saying that we are 'Made in the Image of God' is not a stretch, because the goal of life, of accessing our Higher Self and transcending this earthly plane, is to recognize that God is truly within each and every one of us. "God" is merely the energy of Love, as it vibrates at the highest frequency. The way we can elevate ourselves is by first acknowledging the Love that exists within us and Loving ourselves beyond measure, and it is then that we are able to extend that Love into the world for others, and make a difference at a greater scale.

The lesson of Self-Love is the most important message of all. It is truly a Mastery of Self.

By transcending the traumas of our past and

present lives, we break the repetition of hurt, and the mentality that we are "not good enough as we are." We no longer seek our purpose outside of ourselves, but we find it within us, and it begins with the lesson: we are whole and complete as we are. A purpose that is rooted in loving ourselves is just as important – if not more so – as making a difference in the lives of others. Rising above self-doubt and Mastering ourselves is precisely how we become full and complete, enabling us to point out the Kingdom of God that exists within others who doubt it. The first step is you and your spirit, and that causes a bigger shift in consciousness than you can imagine."

- *Unknown*

LESSONS ON FREE WILL AND DESTINY

"Any true spiritual teacher – even God – is not interested in having your personal power. Rather, the opposite is true; true spiritual teachers are interested in empowering you."

– *Joshua David Stone, Ph.D*

THE TRANSFORMATIONAL PATH

This is a powerful statement, and it often crosses my mind when I am asked to give readings where clients ask for their definitive future, not realizing that's not how the Universe works. When the words "Destiny is Written" are spoken it means that all possible outcomes are available to you, and what path you decide to traverse is your Destiny.

Dr. Brian Weiss discussed this further when he began studying progression therapy which focused on seeing into the future. He asked his patients what their future would look like if they continued with the same habits and struggles they currently had, and then to visualize an alternative future where they eliminated these traumas and healed. That is how Free Will works with relation to Destiny. Will we continue to not learn our lesson in this new lifetime and pick the path that causes us pain and struggle, or will we learn from the lessons of our past lives and our present traumas, and change the course of our future?

Someone asked me, "How does [that] work with people who are victims of horrible crimes - who would choose that destiny for themselves?"

I used my own sexual assault as an example in my response. I did not choose that road in this lifetime (to be sexually assaulted) but my assailant did, I knew he would, and I agreed to this lesson before incarnation. He had the Free Will to choose another path but had chosen this one. I was caught in the crossfire of his Free Will. This is not Destiny that was written for me; I could have learned the same lessons in this lifetime if he had chosen the other path. He chose the path of aggression and I was the victim of that decision. I forgive him for choosing this path.

I told this person that I have likely encountered my assailant in many other lifetimes, and he probably has been given the same choice in numerous lifetimes as well – act with aggression or choose the path of compassion – which causes him to repeat this error in this life. He continues to choose aggression of his own Free Will. My path gets tainted by his decision, but this was not written in my Destiny. My Destiny is the path I choose to traverse after this cruelty. My Destiny is what is written by my own Free Will, no one else's.

And so, my work in spiritual services lays out the same information; here is the outcome you will have if you choose this path, here is what you will have if you choose the other. You make the final decision. You are the one who is given the tools to create your own Free Will, to empower your own life.

So many people are so comfortable in their misery, that the thought of altering the path they are already walking is a burden to them. They'd much rather have the world feel sorry for them and the miserable life "they've been handed," but no. You have chosen to continue down that path. You have chosen to keep the road of victimization and self-loathing and sorrow. You can create the abundant life you wish for yourself if you are given the proper tools to do so, which is what a Spiritual Healer aims to do for you (along with a medical therapist!)

No Spiritual Healer will be your quick fix and no Spiritual Healer will put the work in for you, so if that's what you're expecting, prepare to be disappointed. You are the Master of your own Life and the work comes from you and your hands. You are handed the tools by a Healer and encouraged to start chipping away to reveal your marble self, on your own terms.

Sometimes we hate what we are told – I have had, and heard of, situations where people think the session is an "attack on their character" when really it's just their Healer clarifying where the weaknesses in a person's character, preventing them from having the successful life they deserve. It's not meant to offend. It's not meant to stir ego. It's meant to help a person be their best self. And if it made someone uncomfortable, that should be even more reason to analyze *why*...

What trauma, past life memory or personal insecurity was triggered by this information, and why? How can you use that as a tool to empower yourself and be better? Often we hate what we are told because it means we must begin our marble carving from scratch after we thought we were doing so well! Will you empower yourself with this frustrating information or continue down your path of ego? That choice is up to you. It's not said to you to take your power from you or make you feel small or incomplete, it's said to you to help you better yourself, step into your greatness, and live a life of spiritual grace.

In the end, distrust any healer who says they have all the answers. Distrust anyone who makes you rely on them like a guru and doesn't give you the strength or confidence to venture out on your own. Also take the time to reflect on how the choices you make affect the Destiny you create for yourself. Take time to reflect on where you failed to use the advice, guidance, or information provided by healers because it would have been: too much work, hurt your ego, meant you had to start from scratch, would require you to walk down a different path when you were quite comfortable with the one you were on. Where have you failed to use these tools handed to you because they challenged you and your confidence or the comfort of your sadness?

If you won't walk down your best-self path with your own two feet, don't think your Spiritual Healer will push you down it. Distrust anyone who does, because mastery of yourself is the foundation of all spiritual growth and it can only be achieved on your own.

THOUGHTS ON TOE-DIPPING SPIRITUALITY

What is it?

This is the idea that you have to "do it all" when it comes to your Spiritual Path. It's the new spirituality concept of putting your fingers in all the pie. It often ends up in the study or practice of conflicting paths and leads to burn-out, confusion, loss of identity, or could potentially lead to issues with dark entities.

Apart from just a general human nature of being curious – which often fades away after we take a sniff and say, "No, that's not for me." – Toe-Dipping Spirituality can happen for the following reasons:

1. Power/Control – This is an emotion stirred by the ego, the desire to "Master it all, Learn it all, Be the best at it all," and is usually a push from dark entities and not from the Light. Seeking to control all aspects of Spirituality is the opposite of one of the most important aspects of the Spiritual Journey - non-attachment.
2. Insecurity – The lack of security that you have in your own abilities or your own place within the Spiritual Community. Feeling as though you are not good enough and need to learn it all in order to be respected, validated,

accepted, or trusted. Another cause of insecurity could be from not really knowing who we are; this takes deep healing.
3. Temptation – This ties in slightly with Power, although it comes from a more empty place; being tempted by what power potentially awaits you at the end of the path.
4. "Fads" – This leads back to Insecurity because path-pavers don't follow fads. You only follow Spiritual Fads if you fear your own path or strength to walk it.

We don't need to do *it all*. We all have our one path, unique to us. We need not compare our path to the next person.

Curiosity is not dangerous, but the emotion leading our continuation down the path could be. Ask yourself, "What is the source of you desiring to 'Master it all'?"

Be honest with the answer that comes to you. Conflicting paths confuse our spirit.

ARCHANGEL SANDALPHON - DOWNLOAD

Where do I begin?

"Begin at the beginning. There is no need to contemplate how to start this because it all exists inside your spirit. You merely need to release your grip on getting this perfect and just allow yourself to stream this out as it is meant to be received. You are tapped in and I will do the rest from here. Trust in your ability. Trust in your connection. Trust that I will not lead you astray when you write my word."

Who is speaking?

"Sandalphon."

Why have you chosen to connect with, or through, me?

"Through you is more accurate. Though that is not to say that you are solely tapped in. This is accessible to all if they just allow themselves to listen more carefully. You are not special and I know you know this. We are grateful that you have made it part of your mission to teach this to others. Don't hesitate to continue to share with others how they can access our messages themselves. We like that you have made 'Life Purpose' your focus in your work because we know this message comes clearly through you and helps start a ripple of light.

This is important.

People who are doing lightwork but who are doing it for self-serving means or for their pride, and not to extend the light, are doing us a disservice. What I mean by 'extend the light' is that lightworkers are meant to ignite something in those they work with, that encourages them to step into the world of healing the planetary vibration as well. This is not a solo journey. You are not the solo teacher. Everyone needs to be an active part in this."

We have not communicated before, why have you chosen to speak to me now?

"I am a prophet who has Ascended. You are also a prophet. I could feel that it scared you to write that, but it is not the first time you have been told these words. I know Mary has come to you and said the same. You are a prophet, which is why we are continuously stressing that you write. I can feel you worry that the word 'prophet' comes with 'fame' – something you are not interested in – and potential persecution – something that you fear due to past life trauma. This is a different time. Embrace the name. Wear it boldly and proudly. If it comes from a place of love, rather than ego, it is not something you should fear using.

Prophet merely means one who shares the word of God and that is what you are doing. You are not keeping it for yourself, you are sharing it with others in the hopes of helping them grow and rise. You are teaching others how to also become prophets. It is not an exclusive term. Don't allow human projections onto this term to make you fear it when we gift it to you."

How can I be best for you?

"Write every day, like you are doing now. It is clear that asking us questions, much like you do with the tarot cards, allows you to connect with us better in a way that receives our messages more clearly. Thank you for letting us control your fingers as you write this. Thank you for writing quickly and without a second thought or ego-analysis of what is coming to you. Thank you for being a stream of our energy that allows this download to come forth without hesitation or resistance."

What message do you have for other people who may be reading this?

"That the Kingdom of Heaven is inside all of them and that they can access this wealth of knowledge, just as you do. This gift is not exclusive. It just takes time healing the wounds, blockages, and walls you've set up against receiving it. And it comes more easily to those who seek it out of love rather than out of ego. If you want this connection 'so badly' then analyze where that 'want' is rooted. We will come to you when you want it for love, and to watch the vibration of the planet grow. We will not gift it to you if you seek it out of power or fame.

We are watching carefully how many spiritual people have gone down the path of power and ego and it frightens us, just as it frightens you. People who started rooted in love and became consumed by the 'power' of our connection. There is nothing powerful in this connection. It is not reserved for some. It is not an authoritative stance. It is not meant to put some in a leadership position while others get lost and left behind. This is accessible to all. And if it is accessible to all, it's an equitable gift and there is no power involved. Some people just need help getting to this point of connection.

Others need help finding it again due to being consumed by the ego-rush of initiation. For those, they require a re-initiation. You must break down the entire building and start at the foundation again. It is a re-healing process. You must be careful with how you proceed with these gifts. Starting again will take you 3 times as long to build up to the same trusted level.

Do it right and carefully and lovingly the first time, and all will be well."

Thank you. I am so grateful. Can I share this?

"That is the point.

You are loved.

We are one.

Write.

Write.

Write.

Write.

Write.

Write.

Write. Please. People will listen. This will change the world."

Can you tell me about re-initiation of the gift? Re-reading our conversation has pulled me to ask this. Can we communicate once more before you go?

"Re-initiation begins at the beginning, so it is funny that you ask where you should start. If someone has begun this journey with the right intentions but was thrown off course by the temptation of power, the drive of ego or pride, and a mindset focused solely on wealth – which you know is gifted to you when you do our work, regardless – then you truly must begin again. The journey to the top is harder. You have slipped down the mountain, and the path you first walked is no longer available to you. It is overgrown with vines, with thorns, and full of demons who once consumed you along this first journey. You must choose a new path.

The first path was the easiest path and now you must choose a harder one. To re-ignite the connection and re-initiate the gift we want to share with you, your work into healing the ego that first consumed you is a more difficult task. We must be able to trust you. We must trust that it will not happen again this time around. We gift those who are rooted in love because Love is the energy of God and that is an energy we trust. If you have broken our bond, you have broken our trust. It must be re-earned through re-healing.

It is just like a human relationship! How difficult it is to devote yourself completely to someone who has broken your trust! Monks are a perfect example of this more difficult path of devotion. And what are they gifted with? The purest connection to the gift available to all! How can we not trust those who dedicate, out of love, their entire lives to this work – work on self and work to bring enlightenment to others? We ask the same of those who have fallen. We ask the same hard work.

It's different for all people, depending on how deeply rooted the ego and power became, depending on how many demons must be cleared from their spirit which consumed them with pride. However, it is still an accessible path for all! That is the point. You can be reinitiated many times, but the journey gets more difficult each round.

Learn how to properly root yourself in love, and ground yourself in Spirit, and you won't slip the first time around."

How does one do that?

"You know, but it will be written at a later time. This connection must end. I am consuming you; your vibrations are extensive. You need to rest. This is new for you. We must take it slow. You are loved."

Thank you.

MELCHIZEDEK - DOWNLOAD ON THE FALL FROM GRACE

Melchizedek was weird to connect to. He took a lot of my energy. He vibrates very quickly and he speaks very quickly, so I am sure I missed some of what he was trying to convey to me. He also caused me dizziness and light flashes (with colors). I have never connected with him before, I even had difficulty writing his name, and didn't know anything about him prior to this (despite working with Ascended Masters, he is not one I ever connected with). The download is short because I wasn't energetically prepared.

I was told to write every day, so here I am. Is there anyone from the God Force who wishes to step forward today? What should I write about?

"Let's speak about what you wrote which is 'Fall From Grace' as it corresponds to the message provided by Sandalphon yesterday in which he described slipping down a mountain and having to begin your lightworker journey, once again."

Who am I speaking to?

"Melchizedek"

Why have you come forward?

"Because of where you are located."

What does that mean?

"Paris will be a central hub for healing and I will be at the forefront."

Why Paris?

"Its history has prepared it for this spiritual revolution. Its people are ready. There is no sitting back in silence any longer. Transformation is on the horizon. You call this home for good reason. Your spirit was aware of the work starting here. It is a disaster, it needs a cleanse, the cleanse is happening, people are awakening."

Who are you?

"I am a healer and ultimate teacher, I had an earthly form and now I am Ascended. I am a Master of magic and healing. I use the tools of the hands and geometry to achieve my work."

What message do you have to bring forward?

"That the re-initiation will be a challenge set forth by me. That a Fall From Grace is a perfect description of when one gets caught in the space between light and dark, when one is led forward by ego, by a performance or persona that is not true to their Spirit, by a temptation of power and glory, and a consuming of pride. Grace is the freedom given to you by the energy of Love which is the energy at which God vibrates and to pull from that, which is truly the natural state of all humans, is to fall from Grace. We are only as holy as we allow ourselves to be.

When we are led by our ego we have chosen the less holy path. We must understand that to be like God, we must carry the responsibilities of God and the responsibilities of creation. This vibration carries responsibilities, it is why I am a Master. I too have responsibilities that I must fulfill by acknowledging and receiving this role. I am honored by them. When humans receive this gift of Grace, this gift of Holiness, but then choose to taint it with the dangers and consequence of ego, the fall is hard, fast, painful. To rise again means to struggle more, but I haven't come here to just talk about that struggle. You spoke enough about this yesterday with Sandalphon. I have more messages to bring you."

What messages do you need to bring to those who may read this?

"That the Awakening is now. The shift is now. Step into your responsibilities, step into your soul-governed roles. Work hard to heal your traumas, break and bend the past life lessons, and learn to rise with them. Heal yourself, Master Yourself, love yourself so you can step into the role that has been designated for you, that has been designated for all. You cannot run from what you are made for. You cannot hide from the Awakening. You either step into love with a transcendence of ego or you fall into the pit of darkness and despair. There is no in-between. There is no time for in-between anymore. It is all or nothing.

I know God does not speak in absolutes but the Revelations spoke of the same; it will happen and you will either be ready for it or you will fall. I want everyone to be ready for it. This is not meant to frighten you, it's meant to invigorate you and excite you about the important role you play in this Spiritual Revolution (your readers, not just you, Claudia). You have a job, you have a duty, you are important, you are a key piece in this puzzle.

Will you step into the role you've been assigned, or will pride consume you as you search for a better role, a more important role, a powerful role, a wealth-driven role? Humans know it doesn't matter in the end, right? John Lennon famously said, 'You don't take nothing with you but your soul,' and you don't need to be dead for that to be true.

If you have nothing at all, you still have Spirit, no? If you have everything but feel empty, you've still got your Spirit with you, no? Spirit always. Spirit is the reality. Spirit is love energy and is God. You are God."

How can I help?

"Be fully present when you write. You are tired today. I will leave you. Come back tomorrow with more focus. New projects distract you, among other things. This is the most important project, don't forget this."

Thank you.

THOUGHTS ON THE ASCENDED MASTER JESUS AND DOWNLOAD

I am eternally frustrated by the thought people miss out on the teachings and the love of Master Jesus, simply because his name, image, and purpose has been tainted by Christianity. People eliminate Him completely from their practice likely because of a traumatic history with Christianity (in this life or in a past life). People would rather disregard His existence or His messages completely because of this. He gives them a sour taste in their mouth – but it's not really HIM, is it? It's not HIM that gives the sour taste. It's not HIM that caused the distortion of this message and his image and His Being.

I wish I could rectify this darkness that people hold in their hearts for Him (or Mary, or any historical figures that are tied to His history). He was a radical Jew, named Yeshua, who sought to eliminate religion because He told people, "The Kingdom of God is inside you and you do not need anyone else to get you to that place of enlightenment."

We have The Source inside of us, we are all connected to it. Destroy the leaders who set up restrictive definitions that make getting to that Source as difficult as fitting through the eye of a needle. They are liars. We are all connected, we are all one, Love one another, vibrate on a frequency of Love, know you are worthy, and *you are God*. This message is universal!

Why do so many shun this Ascended Master, this Being of God? I wish I could change their hearts.

As I write this, I am feeling a "frog in your throat" feeling and the same tightness sitting in my Heart Chakra.

I want people to know Jesus as I know Jesus. *What can I do?*

"Remember that the purpose of your being is rooted in the message of Love and that weaves with my own message. We speak the same words but they sound different to the ears of others. They are all rooted in Spirit and that is the point. We are one, and so the hate of me feels like the hate of you. You love me because I am with you and I am you and we are all part of the Source. To hear people turn away from me, is to feel as though they are turning away from you, and turning

SPIRITUAL LESSONS AND CHANNELED DOWNLOADS

away from the God Force and the God within themselves.

You feel as though they are not honouring their ties to the Kingdom by not honouring me, but that wasn't my point. I don't want people to honour me just for the sake of it. I want them to Love me from the depths of their Spirit because they feel called to. I may not resonate for some and I accept that, so too, you must accept that. You must also accept that the same rejection may exist for your messages. That's okay. That doesn't mean you aren't doing your work well enough.

Some souls are not ready. They won't be ready in this lifetime. They will have fragments of your message carried with them into the next lifetime and they will come closer each reincarnation. Then, when they meet your Spirit, when we all sit with The Source at the end, they will say, 'Thank You.'

It won't be in the lifetime where you were living and breathing, and that is okay.

Did you not say that you wanted to live on through Word? Did I not say I am The Word when I was living? My impact was so small when I walked this earth, but look now. I don't mean the way I have been embodied in Christianity – those numbers are meaningless – I mean that Spirits I have stirred who are living according to my True Word: a Word of *love* and *acceptance* and *oneness with Spirit* and *non-judgment* and *freedom* through understanding that we are *all God*. Those living according to my True Word now, years after my physical death, that is magic, that is what matters. Eventually the truth will shift spirits. You do not need to get frustrated because it doesn't happen in front of your eyes, just keep doing your work."

I am speaking to Jesus?

"You have to ask?"

I can feel the hug and embrace and love of your spirit. It consumes me. What messages do people need to hear from you?

"As always, my messages are rooted in Love. I want people to come to me and know they are accepted as they are. There are those who have tainted my words, soaked it in ego and judgment and hate, and I never was that, I never stood for that, I never spoke of that. My Words were oral and so there are distortions in the transfer of my messages. The Gnostic writings are closer to My Truth (the Universal Truth) than all others, but even those must be read with a lens of criticism. The only way to hear my message as it is meant to be heard, is to speak with me directly. I wish to speak with everyone.

I don't want people to fear working with me because

of the blockages that Christianity has made. I don't want anyone to feel like I am not part of their Path. I am a part of All Paths because I am of The Source and they are of The Source, and so we are One rooted in the frequency of Love. I was man; I suffered, I know the suffering of man, I sympathize with it, I was hated for merely existing and speaking my Truth and, more than ever, souls are experiencing the same.

I am here. I am Love, an embodiment of the energy of Love, and I wish to cloak the world with this. I will work with you if you ask it of me. I turn from no soul which calls to me. Even those lost in the depths of darkness, I will pull them out of it. I am the Bringer of Life. I am the Bringer of Light. I am Freedom. I am Enlightenment. You are of the same, let me help you get there."

How can I best show my gratitude to you? How does one work best with you?

"It is almost silly to say because I know many will turn their nose at the word but prayer. Prayer simply means putting light out from your Heart Chakra and speaking with a sort of 'demand' and speaking with pre-prepared gratitude. What I mean is asking for things with a love energy and saying thank you in advance. Instead of saying, 'Please bring me...' say 'Thank you for...'

Make sure that all is cloaked in a white light of love and that it is brought out from the centre of your chest, like a ball you send out into the Universe. Ask me to 'show you…' and I will show you. Ask me to 'Give you…' and I will give you. Ask me to 'bless you with…' and I will bless you.

Prayers are merely affirmation statements with gratitude. Gratitude leads to manifestation. Meditations where you are centred on the heart also help us connect. That is where I sit, in the heart. Not in the third eye, not in the crown, but in the heart. I am your heart centre. I sit there with Mary, my earthly mother, who has Ascended to Spirit with me. She is Universal Love. She is the Universal Mother. She also wants to exist as separate from the image painted of her by Christianity. She is no-judgment, all-Light, all-Love. She is the Holy Mother. She too wants to work with souls on Earth."

What last messages should be shared with those who read this?

"I Am who I Am, as are You. We are. We are Source. We are God. We are trapped in humanness but these bonds and restrictions can be broken. You can be free and can join Spirit, if you Master Yourself. The Masters (Ascended) help with this. I help with Forgiveness. Perhaps that is why you are drawn to work with me as it seems to be your eternal lesson on this planet, in this incarnation. It's meant to be your last, so please learn release.

I am here to help. I am who I am. I am who I am. I am who I am. Let those be your words too (all who read). Reflect on them, meditate with them, speak them like a mantra. You are who you are. What does it mean to you? Reflect carefully on them. They are important.

I am The Word, you are The Word. The Word is God. Word, I am Word, I am Word. The Word is Source. The Word is Spirit. The Word is the Universe. The Word is the God-Energy of All. You are Word. I am Word. I was Word in Flesh, now I am Word in Spirit. I Am, I Am, I Am, I Am.

It's funny that 'I Think Therefore I Am' was so prominent in philosophy – Thought is God Energy, Thought is Creation (you are your thoughts, where your thoughts go your energy goes, you manifest with thought), Creation is God, You are God. You think therefore *you are*. I think therefore *I Am* – *I Am* is God. You are God. We are all the *I am*. We are all connected to that *Source* (Of Creation). We can lose ourselves and lose the connection, but it merely means re-initiation into the right frequency that unites us. Think of it as two drums that are not on-beat. We must find the beat again (the frequency) so that we sound/feel/resonate as coherent. Don't forget who you are and who you are and who you are and who you are. This is a message for all. We Are *One*."

Forever grateful to connect with you, and honored and filled with thanks and love.

"I am just as honored; have you still not registered this? You are a prophet, Claudia. Do you still fail to recognize the ripples you will send through the planet? Do you still under-value your purpose, impact, love? Why do I sit on your altar? Where is the photo of yourself? Honor yourself just as I honor you. Love yourself as I love you. You may not see the ripples but they exist. The light is spreading. You may not live to witness it but know your impact will be huge. Beyond your comprehension. Let go of this self-doubt and need for external validation (or confirmation) of your impact. It's happening. You are rising, as I am Risen. We are One. I love you, I love you, I love you. I am with you."

In closing the connection, I was interrupted with:

"Healer hands, healer words, we are no different, you and I. We are one and the same. Do you see how you heal? You are magic. You are God as I am God as all are God."

SPIRITUAL LESSONS AND CHANNELED DOWNLOADS

I am grateful for this connection, I am so grateful for Jesus's presence in my life, spiritual and otherwise.

MOTHER MARY - DOWNLOAD ON HUMILITY

"Humility is a forgotten art, and yet it is one that is of utmost important on the spiritual path. It is not a competition. Just as no child is loved more in the eyes of a mother, no child is loved more in the eyes of the Universe. We have forgotten what it means to be brothers and sisters and, instead, have seen one another through eyes of hate. We do not see each other as hands to hold to climb a mountain together; we see one another as roadblocks to our own success.

This idea of 'one-upping' when it comes to performances, inauthenticity, and falsehood to grab clients or attention from the social media sphere, is hate masked in play. No one is having fun. Everyone has forgotten that it's the embers that start the fire. Small, smallness, humility, meekness. Misery is found when you exhaust yourself for inauthentic reasons. 'Burnout' is real and it stems from constantly grasping for attention when the focus should be me, my Son, the God force, the

Universe. Your eyes should be 'on the prize'. The prize is ascension. The prize is not 'attention'. Those are merely distractions along the way.

External validation is not a key factor in ascension. I will not, God will not, notice the person who has more followers first. I will not love the person with the most sales the most. I will not grant access to the Kingdom of Heaven (within you) to the person with the most likes. Hogwash! It's all noise. It's all noise to me and it's all noise to your spirit.

Remember when you lived in the moment and didn't have social media? Remember the joy you felt with life, the inspiration you felt about Spirit? It was authentic living and I noticed, and I called you back to the path. Continue to do that. Share to share words (that are not yours and that are yours) but don't worry about the performance. Keep doing your soul-work and we will bring clients to you who need you most.

Keep focused on the goal of healing to help spirits rise and become closer to me, and we will bring you abundance. Keep the focus on the end goal of ascension for you and ascension for all, and don't be distracted by the other noise. Don't worry about numbers. Don't worry about follows. Don't worry about reach. We will hide you in corners where people will find when they are in the darkest of darkness. We will put your embers of Light into the hearths of people's hearts.

Those who need you will find you. Don't worry about that. Worry about Spirit, and only Spirit. Stop the noise. And don't be distracted by the noise of others. Stay humble, stay grateful. You are so loved and your purpose is clear and the rest can fall to the wayside. The rest is unimportant. The rest is off-frequency and will try and shake yours, though you vibrate at the frequency of Love which is the frequency of God. Keep maintaining that, and don't worry about the rest.

I want to share my message of love with the world. I am not an exclusive ascended figure reserved just for those who call themselves Christians. My image has been tainted by man, but I am untainted and pure. I see all the world and its creatures as my children and I am the Universal Mother. My warm embrace can ease the greatest worries. I aim to help raise all my children in the direction of Light and Love, I want all my children to ascend. I work miracles.

My name is known for this, and I want my name to be on all tongues.

I am the Miracle Worker. I place my finger on your third eye and illuminate your Universe. I open all doors when you speak my name with humility and gratitude. I leave no door shut, no one is excluded from my grace. Crawl to me, or run to me, and I will give you the mercy of miracles. Open windows for others to let the light in, and I will open the gates of Heaven within you. You will be consumed by the frequency of Love and the grace of your Mother. I want my name to reverberate beyond the frequency ties of Christianity. I am important. I am the hand that guides. I am Universal Love. I am Mother and Teacher. Call me once and I am with you forever. You don't need to acknowledge me publicly if you fear what my image or face may cause. I hear your heart and that is enough. You will not hide my name once I begin my miracles. You will sing my name and bring others to me, and that is enough. That is enough.

You are tired today and that is because my energetic vibrations in your dreams consumed you. We were working on you in your sleep. Your Higher Self was in training, so to speak. Your sleep was not rejuvenating, it was more like an exercise session, and that is why you feel drained today. We were doing work. You were expanding. You will see the results of your expansion in a few days. Anticipate work, anticipate energetic ascension, anticipate more soul-callings to reveal themselves, anticipate your purpose to be defined with an intensity you could not imagine.

We were working with you so that you could be your best self on planet earth. You don't need to remember the dream because your consciousness does. Your spirit is aware of our dialogue and the exercises we did. Remain humble and grateful. Your gratitude has been well received by the God Force and Universe and we will continue to ensure you are reaping the blessings of your thanks. Stay focused on your journey and don't be distracted by the noise of others. Encourage others to stop comparing paths. Much of what you see is just a lie. Inner work is inside for good reason; it does not need external place cards.

My work today is done. We are One. Speak my name, share my words, be my voice. Return to the focus of forgiveness, don't forget the importance of that. Write about humility because it is important for others to hear this. Don't take a stage when you do it; keep meek. I love you. I love you all."

METATRON DOWNLOAD ON FORGIVENESS

"I am the I AM. The spirit of forgiveness is one that ties back to the message of humility. When we are able to forgive others and release the negative emotion we harbour in our heart-centres, we are not only showing humility in our ability to let go of ego and say, "I am done with this pain," but we are also demonstrating our strength to not let that pain hinder our growth towards something greater. Because truly holding on to hatred, hinders us from our spiritual growth. It does not just mean saying, "I forgive you," it means truly releasing all the deep-set pain that you have buried regarding this person or situation.

Forgiveness is a cutting of a weed that prevents our plant from growing towards the sun. Forgiveness not only releases the other but releases us from the chokehold of those feelings. Because they are truly choking us. The forgiveness must be soul-deep. So deep, that it's no longer a thought that crosses your mind ever again. We can forgive a person but recognize that the actions of that person were not in line with Love; that is their karma to bear. You do not need to carry over the weight of that karma by holding onto resentment. Freedom is what allows growth. Freedom Through Forgiveness."

Who am I speaking to? What more can you tell me about Forgiveness.

"I am who I AM. Let that sit with you and vibrate your spirit. I am WHO I AM. I am the be all and the end all, I am the voice of God, and the strength of the God Force. I am Metatron. I am one with you and one with all, we are the I AM.

When you forgive, my cube is inscribed on your heart to help accelerate the healing. In addition, my cube amplifies the loving frequency that is sent out to the person to release them from your energetic field. When you forgive with me, I help funnel that love which gently energetically pushes the person out of your field and frees you completely.

Forgiveness is the root at which human beings are fed. This is because being born in this body means we are inherently prone to flaws, error, failure. That does not make us less God-Like if we are able to recognize that, seek to rectify that, and also allow ourselves to forgive those who have fallen from Grace. We know it is difficult, as some humans have fallen so far from Grace that they are barely human at the core anymore (for humans at the core are of the Kingdom of God and the living I AM); the dark has consumed them so deeply that they become anti-human, they are an embodiment of darkness.

Except, what challenges darkness? Love. The Light of the Frequency of Love. And so to Forgive means to project this love into the darkness of their spirit and, in doing so, you may possibly save them. You have saved them by merely releasing them with Love. And I know human nature may cause you to think, 'But what if they don't deserve saving?' - if you really are working to ascend and to reach the level of enlightenment you so desire, then you need to come to the understanding that all, even the darkest, need saving. They need it more than you can imagine.

I hear you thinking, 'What if you wish death upon an awful person?' and this makes me laugh because you know what happens after death; you receive a complete freedom from the body and become one with Spirit. There, you are no longer embodied by the darkness you had on earth, but you are made to reflect on what went wrong (terribly wrong) in your human life and how you plan to incarnate in your next to rectify it (your karma).

If you wish death upon your enemy, you wish that he gets to escape from his soul-work in this life for moments – perhaps many – of pure bliss, before entering to repay his karma. If you truly wish your enemy to learn from the horrors they have done on earth, wish them a long life. One where they have to grow (it's never easy or pleasant), heal, and transform. This doesn't eliminate their karma, but it allows them to carry less weight though harder and more suffering work in this life. You are not wishing suffering, you are wishing healing (although healing sometimes carries the weight of suffering if you have a lot to rectify). This is rooted in the energy of forgiveness."

How do I spread the message of forgiveness more effectively?

"You just need to live it. When a thought that is anti-love is felt, forgive yourself, forgive the other it was projected towards, and release. Living on the frequency of love simultaneously connects you to the energy of forgiveness. Forgiveness is what is needed to heal this planet, for there is much that needs to be forgiven. There is so much darkness, so much war, so much strife, so much pain, and the first step to mend the cracks is to forgive those who have caused those cracks. If the power of forgiveness is strong enough, a spirit is shifted, a life path is changed, karmic ties are released, and the planet becomes better.

I know you have fully forgiven your sexual assailant, to the point where you have even released what has

THE TRANSFORMATIONAL PATH

happened to you, believing it to have happened to another body, in another time… a distant memory. In doing so, you have sent the frequency of forgiveness, of love, to your assailant who's name we release as well, and you have shifted him to a path of selflessness, of advocating for others. He has not yet forgiven himself though. His work will have a greater impact once he does, but that is not yours to worry about or your karma to carry. He will carry that into the following lifetime, it is written. You have released and the karmic ties are severed. You have chosen ascension.

Ascension is forgiveness in action. Ascension is the ability to recognize that humanness has flaws but we transcend those flaws to grow."

I am left to think about Cancel Culture… how is this anti-forgiveness?

"Cancel Culture assumes that human beings are perfect, that hatred is not learned but innate, and that someone must be persecuted for being born with this hate. Cancel Culture is the embodiment of the concept of 'original sin' which makes me laugh and shake my head because those perpetuating Cancel Culture, often have a deep-set hate for Christianity!

Cancel Culture assumes we cannot make mistakes and rectify those mistakes. Ascension assumes the opposite; that all mistakes can be healed through karmic energetic exchanges and dedicating your life to God and the energy of Love. We do not cancel you for getting it wrong. We merely encourage you to grow from the start. Re-plant the seeds. Re-water the soil. Feed it with nutrients that help you rise, not stunt your growth. Soak the roots in Love and not in Hate. No dying plant deserves to be tossed without the opportunity to be replanted and re-grow.

Cancel Culture is a disease and those who use it are also masked in the fear that their human errors may also come to the surface. By pointing their fingers at those in the spotlight and screaming *'Canceled!"* they divert the attention away from their own mistakes, errors, discrimination, and *humanness*. Cancel Culture is anti-ascension. Cancel Culture is anti-Spirit and anti-Light. Cancel Culture must be unlearned, just as hatred is unlearned. Cancel Culture is anti-forgiveness and anti-humility."

Is there anything else you wish to share with those who are reading?

"I am the I AM. And I urge those who have difficulties processing the energy of forgiveness to call on me and I will assist them. I will draw my cube on their hearts and I will transmute the resentment they are holding onto into a funnel of forgiveness and a release of the fear attached to forgiveness. I want people to release so that they can grow and ascend. That is all."

Thank you, so very much.

---

1. Weiss, B.L. (1995). *Through Time Into Healing*. Piatkus Books.

"There is nothing noble in being superior to your fellow man; true nobility is being superior to your former self."

- Ernest Hemingway

CHAPTER SEVEN
LIFE, NOW - MY THOUGHTS ON MOTHERHOOD

A s I have previously mentioned, I was able to transition into a state of non-fear as I traversed into my motherhood journey. I do believe that it was a complete trust in the process and non-fear which allowed me to have a very easy and stress free pregnancy. I adored being pregnant and I was generally symptom-free, showering in the joys of the attention that expectant mothers receive in France.

It was a beautiful adventure, one which allowed me nine months to bond, personally, with this spirit inside me. That's a blessing in and of itself that I did not take for granted. I understand what a gift it is for a mother to have nine extra months connecting with this life and, every day, I made an effort to sing to my baby, talk to him, play him music, or interact along with his movements.

Now, of course, life is about balance and, as such, although my pregnancy was a breeze, my labour experience was an absolute nightmare. My birth story did not go the way I had imagined it might go in my head, starting with Pitocin induction - which causes the most painful and horrid contractions that are 30 seconds apart and offer no respite to the mother - and ending in an emergency c-section.

When a c-section was presented to me, my primary thought was for the safety of my child so the decision was a simple one. When I entered the operating room, I knew I wanted my son's entry into the world to be one that was ripe with positivity, laughter, and love - regardless of the screams I was shouting into the Universe moments before my epidural was installed (Pitocin is no joke). I was talking with the doctors and nurses, laughing and generally keeping the spirit of the mood up, showing my fear that it had no place on this path. The nurses even told me and my husband that they'd never seen someone laugh while getting a c-section ("Must be a Canadian thing," they said) and one nurse, Fatima, asked me how I could be so stress-free about the process.

I told her, "I know this is the only option to keep my

child safe. Life has taught me that when there is one decision available as a solution to a problem, stress is a waste of time and energy. Why would I stress about something I cannot change?"

The only time I allow myself to worry is if there are two possible solutions to a problem and I must act quickly, then stress leads me towards a necessary decision - but is short lived. I was presented with the *fact* that a c-section would prevent infection to my baby, so there was no second thought in my head, and no moment of hesitation due to fear. There is one path; I must walk it. Stress and fear have no place on this necessary path.

And so, my boy, Raphaël Ugo Amendola Alzraa, to whom this book is dedicated, came into this world on August 15th 2022 at 4:05 am with perfect Apgar scoring (the doctors wondered why they worried about him at all). They placed him against my skin and I sang to him as he listened to my voice - outside of me - for the first time. And my fairy tale was forever changed, as I was projected down an entirely new path in life - Motherhood.

It's important that I emphasize to you that it really does come naturally; the understanding that this child is yours to protect and nurture, and all other aspects that come along with that fact. Prior to giving birth to my child, I had held one baby. Yes - just one. And it was for a maximum of three minutes, as it started to cry and I panicked. I didn't know how to change a diaper, I didn't know how to hold or dress a baby, I didn't know about the developmental stages of human beings before the age of three, and I certainly didn't know how I would keep this little life alive. However, I just knew that I would be capable.

I know, with certainty, that whether this child came out of me, out of a surrogate, or was adopted and handed into my arms, all these results of "just knowing" would have still hit me. There is an energetic connection that instantaneously occurs that bonds you with this life and allows you to truly *feel* what they need, how they need it, and exactly how to do it.

The spiritual bonding of parent to child, especially, I feel, goddess mother to creation of life, is truly explosive and, like all explosive spiritual experiences, it catapults you through a symphony of emotions. I have decided to capture these in philosophical verse format; short thoughts on spiritual matters related to this journey.

If this book has taught you anything at all, it is how I plan to raise my son and how I believe we can all create a more compassionate and joyful future. I intend to stress to him the importance of being a good person over the importance of being "something of value." I will teach him to pursue his joys and make sure they are joys he defined for himself along the way. I will not let him fall into an over-achiever mentality and will not allow him to be hyper-fixated on checklists. I will lead him with love and teach him forgiveness so that he also extends this into other relationships throughout his life. My dreams and intentions for my son are that he heals all his karmic baggage and grows into an abundant - however he defines that - human. He chose me to be his guide and I will hold his hand when he needs me to. And perhaps this book will be a beacon for him. After all, it is for him.

I am quite positive that one of my final karmic lessons will be that my dual-citizenship son will leave his old mother for Canada when he's a grown man, likely having fallen in love with a Canadian in the process. I am already laughing in anticipation of this lesson from the Universe!

Resisting change is as futile as trying to combat the Universe as it presents you various lessons throughout your life. Anyone who says that the motherhood journey, "doesn't have to change you," or, "needn't change how you live your life," have decided to only traverse the path with one foot, rather than knee deep in the mud of parenthood. This journey completely *transforms* you and, in some ways, it can be overwhelming and terrifying. There is certainly a loss of identity through this change that can make you feel like an impostor or has you reassessing which direction in your life is of the most importance. You will find the compass always returns to this little soul. This little person is the focus of the needle, fully and completely. Anything less feels like an abandonment of the soul that chose you, specifically, for their own journey.

There are many people who will have opinions, criticisms, and commentary to make about your parenting, but the innate connection you have to care for this spirit is beyond their understanding - and far beyond their judgment. Do not lose yourself in the noise of other people's outside opinion on your child's needs. Do not allow them to project in an attempt to show their authority. Asserting yourself and your strength as a parent is important, as is setting boundaries, regardless of who these opinions come from (eg. family, friends, colleagues, etc.). This child is *your child,* and that needs to be respected from those on the sidelines. Trust me, you know what's best for this life. Don't doubt yourself. Don't allow other people to instill that doubt in you.

LIFE, NOW - MY THOUGHTS ON MOTHERHOOD

Your relationship with your partner *will* change and, if you don't have a partner who is willing to carry the same weight as you, you will come to resent them. I was blessed with a husband who had intentions, from the start, to be the best possible father and support system to me. The love for your partner will change drastically as they take on a parent role; it transforms into something more tribal and sacred, rather than sexual and exciting. The bond of *family* that expands with the addition of a little life is so different and so special. It is, fundamentally, spiritual in nature. Although, truly, if you do not have a partner who is willing to help you carry this load, a child will destroy a relationship because everything - absolutely everything - changes in this dynamic.

The primary role of *mother* cannot be understood by anyone outside of the role. Quite honestly, the weight we carry is far greater, the fatigue we face reaches far deeper, and the stresses we have to navigate are way more extreme. No matter how much your partner sits on even ground with you, they cannot understand this role the way you do. And that's okay, so long as you don't blame them or project your frustrations towards them for not understanding.

Your gift of motherhood is profoundly sacred and the bond extends beyond spiritual understanding of anyone other than goddess mother, but all gifts are both blessings and curses. When the weight becomes too heavy to bare, it's okay if you need to pass things on to the second in command - even if they don't navigate this path with as much understanding as you may do. That's not their fault, after all.

It's okay to prioritize your family and your moments with your child. It is not selfish. I quickly discovered the difficulty of sharing myself through my healer business. The routine of a newborn cannot be scheduled (no matter what the *mom-fluencers* say on social media); your life now revolves around whatever spontaneous routine they wish to create, that day.

I knew that it would be difficult, during that newborn period, to continue my spiritual work through Seeking Celestial Grace. I knew I wouldn't be able to carve out silent moments dedicated to client sessions, and I knew that I would either begin to resent my work or resent my baby, and I didn't want to resent either.

While I love my healer and counseling work, I love

my child more. I wanted to honor these moments where my child would be dependent upon me. I had a new life to heal, a new hand to hold and guide through their life lessons, and I wanted to dedicate myself completely to him. Although I had clients lined up waiting for me to come off of my maternity leave, and although I knew this would inconvenience many spirits - and perhaps lead to a lot of my clients seeking new people for this work - I knew what my baby needed: me, fully and completely. So, I wanted to give him that and I paused my spiritual work with an unknown end date, unapologetically.

"Mother" is truly a vocation, much like healer. It's not a job, but it's also not a walk in the park. It requires all of you at all times, and I was happy to give myself to the role. I knew how important it was to my life path and purpose in this moment. This spirit needed me, and I needed him, just as much.

A baby is not a solution to fill the cracks of a questionable relationship foundation. It is not your baby's responsibility to fix, heal, or mend whatever adult traumas haven't yet been healed - within your immediate family or outside of it. You cannot expect a child to come in and make things better where you, a partner, a family member, were unable to put in the work yourselves. If the foundation shakes before a baby enters the picture, expect it to crumble if you don't put in the work before their arrival.

I will touch upon a controversial topic, now. Please note that these comments are unrelated to Postpartum Depression which is a very real, hormonal, overwhelming, and intrusive trauma that requires thoughtful (medical) healing.

There are many mothers who say they resent motherhood and hate being a mom (obviously they don't hate their child, but they hate the role). I believe this resentment comes from an unpreparedness prior to the pregnancy and birth, and unresolved traumas that continue into the motherhood domain. This also comes from over-attachment and an inability to not only move through the necessary stages in your life, but to become resistant to change.

Do you ever notice the friends who say, "High school years were the best years of my life!" are the same people who are unable to manage change, don't do well outside of their old routines, and are resistant even to people growing and developing; sometimes so much so that they cannot manage people becoming different from who they were in high school?

LIFE, NOW - MY THOUGHTS ON MOTHERHOOD

I believe those who say, "I resent motherhood," fall into the same category. Over-attachment to their lives before children, their identity separate from children, perhaps their wildness and chaotic behaviour which needs to be ordered following children. It's almost always something - a pleasure, a characteristic, a passion - that simply didn't benefit them, their spiritual growth, and their ultimate spiritual path on this planet. Because I do believe having a child does push you to become a better person.

It's not a necessary path for people who are able to traverse through this growth on their own terms, but for those who resent motherhood, it's almost always a necessary lesson to propel the growth that, unfortunately, they've seemed to miss. Caring for another spirit who has chosen you with intention as a way to unlearn their karmic lessons and move towards their own life purpose is an immense honor, and there's no other way of putting it.

If you resent this honour, it's because you didn't put in the necessary healing required to carry that weight. What you are truly saying is, "I resent that I needed to put more work into healing and was unprepared for this path. I resent that this path required more from me, more I needed to let go of which I was too attached to."

THE TRANSFORMATIONAL PATH

Birth trauma is very real and, if left untreated (or unfaced, in my opinion), it can become a detrimental factor in your postpartum experience. Sometimes, our births do not proceed as we anticipated, and so many books and videos that you watch as you're pregnant tell you that the only way for a birth to joyfully proceed is for it to be natural with meditative breathing techniques to keep you centered. Adding an epidural is "unnatural" and, worst of all, a c-section is a nightmare way for your child to enter the world!

Of course, now, I realize how stupid all that is.

When we are merely a spirit choosing to enter this life, we also choose how we will enter it. This is an agreement that Spirit Babies have made with their birth; it influences how their life on this planet will proceed, provides lessons to the mother and father, and could even work towards tackling past-life karma that was carried over into this lifetime.

For example, I have quite vivid past-life memories of losing children during childbirth. I believe that everything, from my very painful contractions which gave me horrible nightmares the first night after my birth, the emergency with myself and my child during labour, and the last-minute decision to perform an emergency c-section, were all compounded to give me an opportunity to change the narrative of this birth.

All these instances were certainly traumatic birth

experiences, but I approached them with a calm mindset. I made it clear to my husband that in any emergency situations where it might be me or the child, I fearlessly told him to choose the child. No resentment underlined that decision and I had no worries about what may await me under those circumstances. I very calmly agreed to a c-section without hesitation, knowing it was necessary for the survival of my boy, even though every prenatal video I watched said, "last resort," "not ideal," and, "if you absolutely must," about this birthing option. Throughout the labor, surgery and afterbirth process, I was apologizing if the situation caused any inconvenience in the hospital and thanking all staff members for their dedication to me and my baby's health, smoothing over any energetic ties that may have formed during the entire birthing experience.

In the end, I came to terms with how my birthing experience unraveled and I loved and accepted it because it brought me the greatest gift in my life, my son. In past-lives, I do have memories of resenting the process and it not only influencing how I bonded with my past-life child, but also how I handled the entire postpartum experience. This is how Raphaël decided he would enter the world, and part of accepting him into my new life was accepting how he came to be. Even my friend, Nataskia, who is heavily gifted, told me that he was ready to meet me but would arrive when he wanted to

THE TRANSFORMATIONAL PATH

and on his own terms - and she (or, rather, he) wasn't kidding!

What is interesting, is that he continues to do everything on his own terms, even now. He is developing quickly for his age, he is demonstrating behaviours that make it hard to believe that he is barely three months old (at the time of writing this) and he surprises me every single day. I am grateful for all aspects of my birth, no matter how traumatic they were, because they brought me to where I am, here and now, with my beautiful and incredible son.

In my first few weeks of motherhood, I experienced a loss of identity. All the things I loved and was able to do before this baby, unhindered, were now complicated by feelings such as exhaustion, simple distraction, and lack of time. I couldn't sit down and have thirty minutes of undisturbed work or enjoyment of my passion projects because the baby needed me. I wondered, "Who am I if I can no longer take pleasure in my joys unencumbered?"

However, I realized that my passions were not my identity. When people ask me, "Who are you?" I will not reply, "a book reader, a scrapbook journal lover, an editor, and a content manager," but I will respond, "a mother."

LIFE, NOW - MY THOUGHTS ON MOTHERHOOD

This title is so much more important to my identity because it clarifies that I am patient, I am compassionate, I am dedicated to community betterment, I am working towards raising a soul to be a valued member of society, I am loving, I am selfless, I am creative. These characteristics are so much more important than things I love to do.

And so what if the things I love to do are disturbed? I still have the opportunity to do them, just on an adjusted schedule. I still have years down the line where they will become "easy" to enjoy again and I will be able to share these with my son when he is older. I find way more joy in spending time with my son, chatting with him, adventuring with him, showing him the world, than I ever did from reading a book; and, trust me, I love to read!

I feel it is infinitely more important and valuable to the planet and betterment of mankind to raise a good soul than to sit with my passions. There is so much more that ripples out into the community through my motherhood than through my joy of collecting, reading, or scrapbook journaling. Joy is important because it puts you in an energetic mindset that allows you to be of the greatest value to others. Once you shift the mindset of motherhood from being "freedom sucking" to "karma healing, energetic bond breaking, and transformational," you begin to see how profoundly important it truly is.

THE TRANSFORMATIONAL PATH

The rest fades away like noise and joy overpowers all of your motherhood experience.

With all that being said, it is important that if you are experiencing depression, excessive anxiety, intrusive thoughts, or a general disinterest in your child, it is crucial that you seek out help. As always, I recommend professional medical therapy and spiritual therapy as they create the balance you'll so desperately need during this time. Medical advice will help you work through it, fully and completely. Spiritual guidance will help you heal any traumas from before, during, or after the birth that is making it difficult to connect with your baby.

This little life needs 95% of you, not 5%, and if you give them all of the percentage of you that you can muster, you'll notice a difference. You'll see how their eyes light up when they look at you, you'll notice their developmental advancements (Raph is barely at three months as I write this and you would think he's at a six month level for communication, alone), their trust in you which will be felt through their energy; it's magic and worth every second if your time.

Sometimes life will have to be put on pause to cater to their needs. Sometimes your schedule or routine needs to be adjusted to fit theirs. Sometimes you'll have a sleepless night to soothe their tears. Yet, you will find that the struggles fade into the distance as you witness their growth, feel their love, and heal their spirit through your presence. You will find you don't need sleep when you have a reason to wake up. And, no matter what the books, videos, or mom-shaming social media accounts tell you, you can never hold or love on your child too much; that is *exactly* what this little human needs and craves and, I promise you, you won't regret those moments (you'll only ever regret listening to those who told you not to do it).

This is not meant to be a parenting book so I won't let it transition into that, but just know that I spent years saying I never wanted children and felt that I was truly doing a service to humanity with this position. In the end, this child is my greatest gift and my greatest accomplishment. The lessons the Universe has taught me through this spirit are endless and I've barely had a moment's time with this soul. I cannot even imagine what growth we will both get out of this relationship and bond as the time goes by. My gratitude that this little human chose me to be their mom never goes unnoticed - I thank him every day.

My gifts have shifted as I do feel that my priorities have also shifted. Energetically, I feel intertwined with my son and it is challenging for me to silence that connection in order to tune-in to voices "outside my bubble." I'm not sad about this because I know this will mean that my gifts will likely appear to me in new forms and in unexpected ways. For now, his soul speaks to my soul and that is enough for me.

I am content.

"I've seen you, beauty, and you belong to me now, whoever you are waiting for and if I never see you again, I thought. You belong to me and all Paris belongs to me and I belong to this notebook and this pencil."

- Ernest Hemingway

OUR STORIES NEVER TRULY END

As I write this, I'm still living in the French Alps in a small town called Saint Jorioz. From the front balcony of my house, I can see the snow-tipped mountains.

I'm not sure how much longer I'll be here, exactly, as the adventure always seems to continue. If I continue to approach life with an eager openness and attachment-free mentality when it comes to where these adventures may take place, then I always seem to end up in a location that teaches me even more about life and about myself. Every spot we've moved to has been beneficial to my growth and monumentally important in my journey. While I love it here and think this is an ideal place to raise my baby boy, I also know that maybe it's not what *he* needs, and trust that life will take me where *he* needs to be.

I want to remind you, yet again, that comfortable is not a synonym for abundant. Ticking off items from your life checklist will not bring you joy if you are endlessly fixated on what sits next on that list. If you notice that your "monumental accomplishments" do not seem to bring you the joy that you were promised, listen a little closer to what your heart is asking for. Then, put in the work to give it what it wants.

This will always come with risk, discomfort, and potential financial downfalls, but, I promise you, when the Universe realizes the trust you've put in it, it will reward you in the ways that matter most: through endless happiness and a love-filled life.

Mute the nay-sayers and negative Nancys and listen very carefully to the whispers of your Spirit. It's the one that truly knows what's best for you and everything in life will try to pull you off that path. Because, can you imagine a world filled with endlessly joyous and fulfilled people? Consumerism culture would fail, life coaches would lose their livelihood, unhealthy foods you reach for when you're depressed would sit untouched on grocery store shelves. This world and its economy thrive on people being sad and unfulfilled; how else can they market so much of what you really don't need?

Living joyously and manifesting a true abundant life

for yourself is the most counter-culture thing you can do. It's also the path that will lead you to the greatest personal betterment, making you an even more valuable member of your community.

I hope my journey has inspired you, and I hope my many hard lessons have been eye-opening for healing your own life. Simply by reading this book, our paths are intertwined; you have helped to support my dream of being a writer and have energetically contributed to my fairy tale life of joyful abundance. For this, *I thank you.*

I hope you will take a moment to find and share with me how you are taking the steps to transform your own life.

Know this: I believe in you, and you deserve your own fairy tale life. Abundance is your birthright, so walk the transformational path that awaits you.

ABOUT THE AUTHOR

Claudia Amendola Alzraa is a bibliophile, logophile, and Francophile. She lives driven by joy and filling her life with passion. Nothing quite compares to a lazy Sunday with her husband, son, and Australian Cattle Dog, Poe.

When she's not reading, creative journaling, or writing, she's lending her clairaudient mediumship abilities to others through her spiritual business Seeking Celestial Grace©. She offers life purpose tarot readings, spiritual counseling, and Higher Soul Consciousness Readings, where she goes into the origin of your soul and theorizes the lessons presented to her, for you to gain the Awareness necessary to make change or manifest the Earthly experience that you desire. She truly believes everyone deserves to live their most abundant life, and her spiritual work is evidence of that.

Apart from working in - and being enamoured with - the role of Stay-At-Home-Mom, she is also an editor, freelance writer, and content manager for various clients.

She is an Aquarius sun, Leo moon, and Libra rising.

Instagram: @seekingcelestialgrace
Website: seekingcelestialgrace.com, lifeofcloud.net
Email: seekingcelestialgrace@gmail.com

www.ingramcontent.com/pod-product-compliance
Lightning Source LLC
Chambersburg PA
CBHW041308240426
43661CB00038B/1467/J